TRACING YOUR
IRISH FAMILY
HISTORY ON THE
INTERNET

FAMILY HISTORY FROM PEN & SWORD BOOKS

TRACING YOUR IRISH FAMILY HISTORY ON THE INTERNET

A Guide for Family Historians

CHRIS PATON

Pen & Sword
FAMILY HISTORY

First published in Great Britain in 2013 by
PEN AND SWORD FAMILY HISTORY
an imprint of
Pen & Sword Books Ltd
47 Church Street
Barnsley
South Yorkshire
S70 2AS

ISBN 978 1 78159 184 0

A CIP catalogue record for this book is
available from the British Library

Typeset in 10pt Palatino by Mac Style, Driffield, East Yorkshire
Printed and bound in the UK by CPI Group (UK) Ltd, Croydon, CR0 4YY

Pen & Sword Books Ltd incorporates the Imprints of Pen & Sword
Aviation, Pen & Sword Family History, Pen & Sword Maritime, Pen
& Sword Military, Pen & Sword Discovery, Wharncliffe Local History,
Wharncliffe True Crime, Wharncliffe Transport, Pen & Sword Select,
Pen & Sword Military Classics, Leo Cooper, The Praetorian Press,
Remember When, Seaforth Publishing and Frontline Publishing.

For a complete list of Pen & Sword titles please contact
PEN & SWORD BOOKS LIMITED
47 Church Street, Barnsley, South Yorkshire, S70 2AS, England
E-mail: enquiries@pen-and-sword.co.uk
Website: www.pen-and-sword.co.uk

CONTENTS

GLOSSARY

Anglican	pertaining to the Church of Ireland
BMDs	births, marriages and deaths
ebook	electronic book
FHL	Family History Library (Church of Jesus Christ of Latter Day Saints)
GRO	General Register Office
IGI	International Genealogical Index
JSTOR	'Journal Storage' (academic ebook resource)
NAI	National Archives of Ireland
NLI	National Library of Ireland
NUI	National University of Ireland
OS	Ordnance Survey
Partition	the division of Ireland into Northern Ireland and the Irish Free State in 1921
PDF (.pdf)	Portable Document Format – a data file format requiring an Adobe-based reader programme to access
Podcast	a digitally based audio or video file which can be downloaded to your computer to view or listen to
PRONI	Public Record Office of Northern Ireland
Quaker	pertaining to the Society of Friends
Tweet	a message sent on the Twitter social network
UCC	University College Cork
UK	United Kingdom
URL	'Uniform Resource Location' – a website address

PREFACE

The idea for this book arose from a deliberate omission in a previous work for Pen & Sword, *Tracing Your Family History on the Internet*, where for reasons of space I had to confine the discussion to the online resources of the United Kingdom. While this included some resources for Northern Ireland, it did the whole of Ireland something of an injustice. This was something that I was particularly keen to redress, not least because both my wife and I are from the island ourselves (from Counties Antrim and Kilkenny), but also for the simple fact that the level of interest in Irish family history research has mushroomed over the last few years.

One of the joys of family history research is the discovery of the unexpected. In my own case, my findings have been often extraordinary, sometimes hilarious, occasionally outrageous, but never dull. When you tell your friends that you are thinking about researching your Irish ancestry, however, the chances are that they will immediately offer their condolences and pull an Oscar-winning facial expression of pain. The received wisdom is that there is absolutely no point in going near Irish research, for there are apparently no records: 'Sure, weren't they all burned in the Civil War?' The short answer is no, they most certainly were not, but the destruction in 1922 of the Four Courts in Dublin, where much of the public record was held, was certainly disastrous. A great deal of material was lost, among the most useful for genealogical research being many parish and probate records, as well as several pre-1901 Irish censuses. A lot was indeed destroyed – but much has certainly survived. Think of the glass as half full and not half empty, and you will be in with half a chance of actually getting somewhere.

In Britain and elsewhere, when carrying out research, some people go no further than consulting the vital records and censuses, but in Ireland you may need to become a little more creative. In some cases it is not to Ireland you should look for resources at all, but to the areas where the Irish emigrated. A useful tip when trying to go through a brick wall is to stop banging your head against it, step back and perhaps try to walk around it. Where a record for a particular family may not have survived, it may well be found for a sibling. You may initially be dismayed to learn that your ancestor had fifteen siblings – but fifteen siblings may mean fifteen chances to solve a problem. Nowhere is it more important to research the entire family, and not just your direct line, than with Irish ancestry.

A great deal of Irish-based research material is increasingly being made available online, thanks to the pioneering efforts of government bodies such as the Public Record Office of Northern Ireland and the National Archives of Ireland, commercial sites such as FindmyPast Ireland and Ancestry, and the zealous activities of bodies such as the Church of Jesus Christ of Latter Day Saints. There is also a massive volunteer community within and beyond Ireland, with many wonderful projects being enthusiastically pursued, while local archives are increasingly adding to the pot also.

The intention of this book is to offer information on many of the key repositories online that can help with your research, to provide tips on their usage, and where possible a few pointers on how to save on costs. I have looked at the whole of the island for resources affecting both Northern Ireland and the Republic of Ireland. From 1801 to 1921 the whole island was a constituent part of the United Kingdom of Great Britain and Ireland, and the British dimension will also be explored.

As Ireland is smaller than Britain, the subject of my previous work, I have a bit more space in this edition to explore many of the sites under discussion. This is therefore not just a book listing websites, but hopefully a more fully fleshed-out work on how to carry out Irish research. Not everything can be done online, and some resources may never make it on to the internet. In the midst of writing this guide I happened to visit Carrick-on-Suir Heritage Centre in County Tipperary and was surprised to discover a series of pawn-shop books from 1864 to 1868 for the town in a locked glass cabinet, listing thousands of occurrences of the town's poorest folk seeking a few pennies here and there for their most prized possessions. I was thankful to be given permission to examine them, and after many hours of study I found several new family members not heard of before, and much about those already discovered. The internet is most definitely not the be all and end all of your research, and the island of Ireland is full of nooks and crannies offering such golden genealogical gems – but be in no doubt, the internet will certainly help provide you with one heck of a starting point.

As with my previous book, it is worth pointing out that the internet is a fast-moving river, and that occasionally sites do get washed up on the banks before making their way to a digital heaven. In some cases it is possible to visit websites that no longer exist, if the pages have been 'cached' by an internet library. Sites that offer such a facility include the Internet Archive's 'Wayback Machine' at **http://archive.org/web/web.php** and the British Library's UK Web Archive at **www.webarchive.org.uk**. Once again, I have also occasionally truncated absurdly long website addresses to an easier-to-type version using the Tiny website at **http://tinyurl.com**.

Where mention is made of fees for commercial services offered online, the rates quoted will be in the relevant currency, depending on the service in question. The currency of the Republic of Ireland is the Euro (€), while that of Northern Ireland and the rest of the United Kingdom is the pound sterling (£).

Once again a huge thank-you must go to Rupert Harding and the team at Pen & Sword for both commissioning this handbook and for their assistance throughout its production, in particular to Sarah Cook for her skilful editing of the manuscript. A huge thank-you must also go to the good folk across Ireland (and abroad) for making Irish family history resources increasingly accessible for everyone. In particular, thanks are due to Brian Donovan at Eneclann, to Bernadette Walsh at Derry City Council's Heritage & Museum Service, to Corporal Andrew Lawlor at the Military Archives at Cathal Brugha, to the Garda Museum in Dublin and to the Police Service of Northern Ireland Museum in Belfast.

As ever, a huge amount of gratitude is also due to my wonderful wife Claire, and sons Calum and Jamie. And finally, here's a glass to the good folk of Piltown and my own native Carrickfergus – cheers and sláinte to both!

The old promenade at Carrickfergus.

PROMENADE, CARRICKFERGUS

Chapter 1

GATEWAYS, INSTITUTIONS AND NETWORKS

Information for the family historian can come in all shapes and sizes, and with various degrees of accuracy. It is therefore worth bearing in mind that the information you obtain from any genealogical source should always be questioned, no matter how obvious or accurate it may seem, and corroborated where possible. It is not always correct to assume that because a record is there in black and white it must be true. Is the information in an original document accurate? Has a transcription been made correctly or fully? Records can contain innocent errors, but they can also be deliberately misleading. A child born illegitimately may well have claimed a mythical father in a marriage record to spare the indignity of such a 'stigma' being recorded again. You might also be surprised to discover just how many people do not age by ten years at a time between regular decennial censuses. Was this due to vanity, or the simple fact that the subject did not know his or her age? Remember that any record found is only as good as the informant or the transcriber who presented it.

Another common pitfall for some people beginning their research is to assume that because they have found somebody with the right name in a record collection, in the desired location and at the right time, they must have found the right person. This is not always the case; there may well have been ten Billy Smiths or Paddy Murphys in the same town, and it may not always be possible to work out which was which. In many cases your research may be as much about 'killing off' possible contenders as it is in bringing back life to your own ancestors.

A particularly useful resource for Irish research is the oral record, the tales passed down through generations from one family member to another. Often the preservation of such stories can help to unlock tricky research problems, but again be wary. It may well be that a branch of the family emigrated to the United States following the Famine – but it may equally be that the Famine had absolutely nothing to do with it, and that the move was made for another reason that has long since disappeared from the folk memory.

Recording information

No matter which websites you consult, keep a note of their addresses and what information you have gleaned from them. You can save website addresses on your browser's 'Favourites' tool, saving you having to retype the addresses on future visits. Be aware that some may change from time to time, particularly with those from local council authorities, and that information remains online in most cases only so long as the host platform is still around, or while the person who created the resource is maintaining it.

It is always advisable to make a copy of any information discovered as soon as you find it. You can type out relevant portions, cut and paste text, save the web page as a file to be consulted offline, print off the page, or take 'screen grabs' (using your 'Print Screen' button).

Gateway sites

There are many so-called 'gateway sites' which can assist in the location of online collections that may help with your research. Some of these host records, while others link to other platforms, meaning that occasionally dead links may appear. Should this happen, it is worth searching for the named collection on a search engine such as Google to see if it might be available in another format elsewhere.

The *Irish Times* newspaper's Irish Ancestors site at **www.irishtimes. com/ancestor/index.htm** is a highly useful platform created by Dublin-based genealogist John Grenham. Although parts of the site charge for some of the facilities offered, it does have some exceptionally useful resources that are freely available, such as the 'Placenames' tab, which allows you to locate the parish of a particular place of interest and to view it on a map. The 'Browse' area is the real workhorse of the site, however, allowing you to identify record collections which may exist for a particular area, including shelf-marks for library holdings and archive-held records, detailed lists of civil and Roman Catholic parish maps and more. A useful site map is also located at **www.irishtimes.com/ancestor/ sitemap.htm**; this can readily take you to the area of interest without going through the menu-based tabs. John's dedicated genealogy blog at **www.irishtimes.com/blogs/irishroots** is also well worth bookmarking.

Jane Lyons' From Ireland at **www.from-ireland.net** offers a similar range of resources for free, and is the result of a research effort first started in 1996. Many record sets are completely transcribed, and the site also contains thousands of photographs and inscriptions taken in graveyards across the island. The various collections are accessible by following the grey links on the 'Explore' bar in the middle of the screen.

Several other sites provide county-based lists of transcribed records. These include the Fianna site at **www.rootsweb.ancestry.com/~fianna/**, Fáilte Romhat at **www.failteromhat.com** (particularly useful for Cork) and Ireland Genealogy Links at **http://tinyurl.com/6xedpwl**. The A Little Bit of Ireland site at **www.celticcousins.net/ireland** has a handful of all-Ireland resources, but is especially useful for Counties Galway, Limerick, Clare, Mayo and Roscommon. The Irish Genealogical Project is another exceptional effort available at **www.igp-web.com**, as is The Irish Archives at **www.theirisharchives.com**.

The World GenWeb project (**www.worldgenweb.org**) has two Irish platforms, located at **https://sites.google.com/site/northernirelandworld genweb** for Northern Ireland and **www.irelandgenweb.com** for the Republic. Both are also accessible through the Ireland and United Kingdom GenWeb Project site at **www.iukgenweb.org**. Each county has transcribed resources and dedicated mailing lists which are well worth subscribing to. There are similar projects available in the form of

The Irish Archives, a useful gateway site.

GENUKI at **www.genuki.com** and the UK and Ireland Genealogy Search site at **www.ukisearch.com**, while the US-based Cyndi's List site is also worth visiting at **www.cyndislist.com**.

The Irish Genealogy Toolkit site at **www.irish-genealogy-toolkit.com** offers a few links to some online resources, but its real value lies in acting as a detailed encyclopaedia to help explain several types of records that may help with your research, with many worked examples. For an overview of many historical topics in Ireland, with links to many heritage sites and a fairly decent history of the island, visit Oracle Ireland at **www.oracleireland.com**.

Irish archives

There are several major institutions within Ireland, from national- and county-based archives to university collections, which have valuable online resources and which you will, in all likelihood, need to visit at some stage during your research. All are now committed to try to make some of their holdings accessible online, albeit to varying degrees.

The key national institutions responsible for the gathering of civil registration records for births, marriages, civil partnerships, deaths and adoptions are the General Register Offices for Northern Ireland and the Republic of Ireland, located in Belfast (**www.nidirect.gov.uk/gro**) and Roscommon (**www.groireland.ie**). Prior to Partition there was a single GRO for the whole of Ireland in Dublin, with civil registration having been implemented on the island in two stages (in 1845 and 1864). There are various ways that you can access their records online, which will be more fully discussed in Chapter 3. For details of local district registration offices in Northern Ireland, where many events are initially registered before copies are transmitted to Belfast, visit **www.nidirect.gov.uk/district-registrars-in-northern-ireland**. The equivalent for local civil registration offices in the Republic are listed at **http://tinyurl.com/3ltebdz**.

The national archive for the north is the Public Record Office of Northern Ireland (PRONI), based at Titanic Quarter in Belfast. Its fairly comprehensive website at **www.proni.gov.uk** offers several useful resources, from free to access digitised records databases and handy research guides to an all-important records catalogue. Among its digitised databases are the 1912 Ulster Covenant, various freeholders' records from across the province of Ulster, online probate resources, photographic resources and more, located within the 'Online Records' section of the website on the top right of the home page.

Also located on the right-hand side of the home page are two further important categories, 'Guides and Leaflets' and 'Search the eCatalogue'.

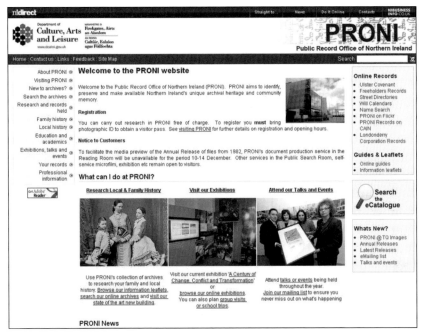

The Public Record Office of Northern Ireland website.

The guides section mainly provides links to downloadable PDF documents, including the important *PRONI Guide to Church Records*, and to more specific topics such as newspapers that can be consulted at the facility, privately deposited collections and more. The leaflets section contains a useful series of downloadable background documents to a range of subjects including local history and emigration.

PRONI's eCatalogue contains detailed descriptions of well over a million and a half items within its holdings. In some cases these can be extremely detailed, containing entire transcripts of letters and various other resources, so it is always worth doing a name search for your relatives within it. The catalogue can be both searched and browsed.

At the time of writing PRONI has yet to fully engage with online social media platforms, but has embraced two particular innovations. The first is the 'PRONI on Flickr' pages at **www.flickr.com/photos/proni**, which contains over 800 photographs from the Allison Collection, depicting portraits and group images from across the country. The second is the use of the YouTube media platform at **www.youtube.com/user/PRONIonline** to present recorded lectures given at the facility to a more international audience.

The equivalent archival repository for the Republic of Ireland is the National Archives of Ireland (NAI). Unlike PRONI, which has so far been aiming to digitise materials 'in-house', the NAI has instead within recent years elected to work with partner agencies to try to make some of its holdings accessible online. Perhaps the most important Irish resources to appear on the internet in the last few years have been the digitised 1901 and 1911 censuses (see p. 62), which were created in partnership with the Ottawa-based Library and Archives Canada (see p. 149). More recently, a collaboration with FamilySearch (see p. 24) has seen additional collections such as probate records appear on the archive's own website at **www.nationalarchives.ie** and from November 2012 on a new dedicated digitised records platform at **www.genealogy.nationalarchives.ie**. A partnership with the commercial FindmyPast Ireland organisation (see p. 12) has also helped to make several other valuable collections appear on the net, most notably the Irish petty session records and landed estates records.

In 2012 the NAI also announced that it had revamped its main website, resulting in a much slicker-looking platform. Several freestanding databases that were previously available, however, disappeared overnight, having been integrated into the new catalogue. The catalogue is

The National Archives of Ireland.

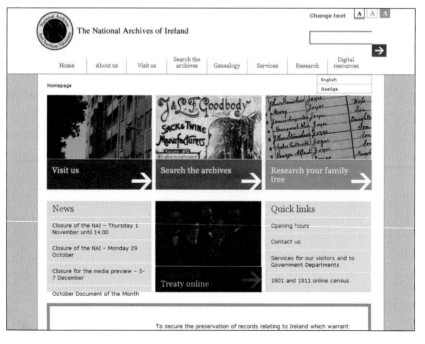

nevertheless a long overdue and very welcome resource, listing items predominantly generated by the Irish Government and the courts, but also acting as the gateway to some of the archive's digitised records.

Like the PRONI site, the NAI pages also include useful resource guides, which are located under the 'Genealogy' tab at the top of the page. The 'Digital Resources' section of the site, accessible from the top menu, leads to a range of stand-alone web-based projects. These include the 1901 and 1911 census website (see p. 62), various online exhibitions, and a dedicated site hosting the Chief Secretary's Office Registered Papers (**www.csorp.nationalarchives.ie/index.html**), a five-year project to place online the registered papers of the Office of Chief Secretary of Ireland from 1818 to 1852.

To find collections within the island's various city- and county-based archives you can visit the site of the repository itself or utilise the Irish Archives Resource website at **www.iar.ie**. Launched in early 2011, this provides a consolidated search platform for resources held by the Irish Capuchin Provincial Archives, Cork City and County Archives, Dublin City Archives, the Guinness Archive, the Irish Film Archive, the Irish Jesuit Archives, Limerick City Archives, NUI Galway JHL, the Public Record Office of Northern Ireland, the Royal College of Physicians of Ireland and UCC Boole Library Archives, as well as the county-based archives for Carlow, Clare, Donegal, Dublin (Fingal County Archives), Galway, Longford, Louth, South Tipperary, Waterford, Wexford and Wicklow. Direct links to the participating archives are located at **www.iar.ie/Links.html**.

A similar platform, which concentrates on library- and university-based holdings, is the Research and Special Collections Available Locally (RASCAL) site at **www.rascal.ac.uk**. Initially designed for Northern Ireland, it was created as a means to provide information on various research and special collections held by Queen's University Belfast, the University of Ulster, the Library and Information Services Council (Northern Ireland), the Public Record Office of Northern Ireland, the Linen Hall Library and Belfast Public Libraries. It has since been extended to cover the whole of Ireland, and now details holdings of the Royal Irish Academy, University College Cork, Trinity College Dublin, Dublin City Public Libraries and many other repositories. A full list of participating institutions can be found at **www.rascal.ac.uk/?func=aboutUs**, via the 'Institutions' tab on the left of the page. The 'Links' page also provides access to many of the partners' sites directly.

Another handy way to identify where many of the island's archives are located is to use the Irish Archives Map, a Google Maps-based interface created by Learn About Archives (**www.learnaboutarchives.ie**), which geo-tags the locations of archives and provides contact details for each. It can be directly accessed at **http://tinyurl.com/d3q6x5c**. Elsewhere, Archives Ireland (**www.archives.ie**) offers details about various repositories but also provides information on professional archive bodies, relevant legislation affecting Irish-based archives (including Freedom of Information details), and more.

British archives

Ireland was part of the United Kingdom from 1801 to 1921, meaning that many British repositories can be equally important for your research. The National Archives (TNA) based at Kew, near London, is the main archive for the UK, predominantly carrying material from England and Wales. Its website at **www.nationalarchives.gov.uk** contains various research and resources guides, as well as a phenomenal amount of digitised material, accessible through the new 'Discovery' catalogue which was introduced in 2012.

In addition to the various military and other records generated by the British state, there are several resources specifically dedicated to the administration of the whole of Ireland during its membership of the UK. These include materials relevant to the Easter Rising of 1916, the records of administration from Dublin Castle, and service records for members of the Royal Irish Constabulary. The body also holds State Papers collections detailing the archives of the various Secretaries of State for Ireland from 1509 to 1782, an important collection that acts as a substitute for many pre-1790 Dublin Castle papers which were lost in 1922 during the destruction of the Public Record Office in the city. A general overview of these records is available via **http://nationalarchives.gov.uk/records/atoz/i.htm**.

Northern Ireland remained within the UK after Partition and so the institution's site can also help to locate many more recent Ulster-based resources. For example, a search for 'Belfast' in the Hospital Records Database at **http://nationalarchives.gov.uk/hospitalrecords** returns information on the location of hospital records for twelve separate medical institutions in the city, from the Royal Victoria Hospital to the Northern Ireland Hospice.

Although the National Records of Scotland, the equivalent institution for Scotland, is predominantly concerned with records for that country alone, its catalogue at **www.nas.gov.uk/onlinecatalogue** is also worth searching for records detailing Irish connections.

More locally, many British county-based archives and other repositories have had their catalogues placed online, with the Access to

Archives (A2A) website a useful port of call at **www.nationalarchives. gov.uk/a2a** for England and Wales, and the Scottish Archive Network at **www.scan.org.uk** for Scotland. For records collections in private hands or in other institutions, you can consult the catalogues of the National Register of Archives at **http://nationalarchives.gov.uk/nra/default.asp** or the Scottish equivalent at **www.nas.gov.uk/onlineRegister**.

Libraries

Dublin's National Library of Ireland (NLI) has a website at **www.nli.ie** with a range of useful materials online for genealogical research. The main home page has various sections, the most important of which is the 'Family History Research' area, which offers a great deal of advice for those planning a visit to the institution. There are several downloadable guides, including an introductory research guide and several detailed 'ready reckoners' to help identify which holdings are available at the facility on microfilm, particularly informative for parish- and land-based resources. Perhaps the most useful tools for the Irish genealogist are the Roman Catholic parish records that are held on microfilm, which in November 2010 the library announced that it was hoping to digitise and make available online in due course.

The NLI site contains many other areas accessible via a menu bar along the top of the page, the most useful of which is the 'Catalogues & Databases' section. Within this you will find the 'Online Catalogue', which includes electronically added records from 1990 onwards, with earlier handwritten entries continuing to be added also. The 'Sources' database is another particularly handy area, with 180,000 records listed, sourced from manuscripts and periodicals catalogued up to the 1980s, manuscripts held in other repositories in Ireland and overseas listed from the 1940s to the 1970s, and material from over 150 Irish periodicals catalogued up to 1969. The NLI has a presence on Flickr, Facebook and Twitter, with links to each at the top of each page on the site, as well as a blog at **www.nli.ie/blog** and a YouTube channel at **www.youtube.com/ user/NationalLibraryNLI**.

Many of the Republic's county-based libraries have contributed ebooks to the Ask About Ireland website at **www.askaboutireland.ie/reading-room/digital-book-collection/**. For additional online resources that they offer, consult Chapters 5 to 8.

There is no national library for Northern Ireland, but two key repositories with a great deal of resources are Belfast Central Library and the Linen Hall Library. The website for the former at **www.ni-libraries.net/libraries/belfast-central-library/** unfortunately provides little more than contact details and opening hours information. The site's page on 'Heritage Collections' repositories based at libraries across the province does include a small PDF document listing some useful books on early twentieth-century Irish history, albeit almost exclusively titles based on political and military history. The main parent site at **www.ni-libraries.net** provides contact information on libraries across Northern Ireland.

The Linen Hall Library, initially founded in 1788 as the Belfast Reading Society, is the last remaining subscribing library in Ireland, and has a much more substantial presence online at **www.linenhall.com**. The 'Collections' category on the site holds detailed guides to many holdings of the institution, including a handful of digitised ebooks, information on its 'Irish and Reference' section, a summary of its genealogy- and heraldry-based holdings, and guides to both its Northern Ireland Political Collection and the Theatre and Performing Arts Archive. Also of immense value is an online catalogue, offering search options by keyword, title, author's name or journal title.

The British Library in London may also offer assistance at **www.bl.uk**, and likewise the National Library of Scotland in Edinburgh at **www.nls.uk**. The National Library of Wales (Llyfrgell Genedlaethol Cymru), based in Swansea, acts as both a national library and a national archive for the Welsh, and is online at **www.llgc.org.uk**.

Heritage
The National Inventory of Architectural Heritage at **www.buildings ofireland.ie** is an interesting website which allows a search of two key ongoing surveys carried out by the Irish Government: the 'Building Survey' and the 'Garden Survey'. These provide key examples of many historic properties and are accompanied by resources such as aerial photographs and maps. An 'Archaeological Survey Database' can be found at **www.archaeology.ie**.

The Northern Ireland Sites and Monuments database is at **www.doeni. gov.uk/niea/other-index/content-databases/content-databases-ambit.htm**, while a separate Buildings at Risk register is available at **www.doeni. gov.uk/niea/other-index/content-databases/content-databases-barni.htm**.

Societies
There are several genealogical and historical societies in Ireland, with many offering useful online holdings and listings. On the genealogical front the island is fairly fragmented, with various independent societies falling under different umbrella groups.

The Council of Irish Genealogical Organisations (**www.cigo.ie**) is an umbrella group which has several participants among its membership, the details for which can be accessed in the 'Constituent Organisations' page. The most useful part of its website for non-members is the 'Links' page, as this provides a fairly detailed list of agencies and records categories covering everything from 'Adoption' to 'Workhouses'.

The Irish Family History Foundation is a cross-border coordinating body for several county-based genealogy centres across Ireland, and hosts an online platform at **www.rootsireland.ie** for their transcribed records, which are accessible for a fee (see p. 17).

Established in 1990, the Genealogical Society of Ireland has a dedicated research and archive centre, An Daonchartlann, based at Carlisle Pier in Dún Laoghaire. Its website at **www.familyhistory.ie** hosts indexes to its journals from 1992, as well as its monthly news-based *Gazette* from 2006, the latter being freely available to read online.

The North of Ireland Family History Society (**www.nifhs.org**) is the umbrella body for family history societies in Northern Ireland, with branches based in Ballymena, Belfast, Coleraine, Fermanagh, Foyle (Derry), Killyleagh, Larne, Lisburn, Newtownabbey, North Armagh (Portadown), North Down and Ards (Bangor), and Omagh. Some of the societies have their own websites, while others use the main umbrella site to advertise their activities. One of the more useful functions on the main site is a search engine that tracks fifty-eight different sites of interest to those with Irish connections. The society also provides addition services to its members, such as a look-up service for graveyard inscriptions at **www.nifhs.org/lookups.htm**.

The Ulster Historical Foundation, formed in 1956, is based in Belfast and has a considerably well developed online presence at **www.ancestryireland.com**. The site offers a range of transcribed records on a commercial basis, but an interesting free offering is an app for Apple- or Android-based mobile devices, which accompanies a driving tour around 200 locations of interest to Ulster-Scots history. Its ebooks page also offers several downloadable publications, some for a fee and others free of charge.

There are two main umbrella groups for local studies societies: the Federation for Ulster Local Studies Limited at **www.fuls.org.uk** and the Federation of Local History Societies (Conascadh na gCumann Staire Áitiúla) at **www.localhistory.ie**. Each website links to member sites across Ireland, providing a great deal of useful resources for historical research.

For those looking for professional assistance, there are a few options. Several genealogists across Ireland are members of the Association of Professional Genealogists in Ireland (**www.apgi.ie**), the Society of Genealogists of Northern Ireland (**www.sgni.net**) or the Association of Ulster Genealogists and Record Agents (**www.dennisirwin.f2s.com/augra/ home.html**). The Public Record Office of Northern Ireland also offers a list of independent commercial researchers at **http://tinyurl.com/cqj3b6k**, as does the National Archives of Ireland at **http://tinyurl.com/76adwzm**. It is worth noting that many family history societies and Irish Family History Foundation-affiliated research centres across the island also offer research assistance.

Commercial vendors

Family history is a fairly competitive business for commercial vendors, offering a vast range of genealogically useful online materials either by subscription or on a pay-per-view basis. This section provides some generic information about the largest organisations which will be referred to throughout the book.

There are a few tips worth taking note of with regards to subscriptions to some of the sites. Many offer an introductory period for free, for which you will need to register with your credit card details. It is worth making sure when you do so that you fully understand their terms and conditions, particularly if you work as a professional genealogist. Also note that some vendors take credit card details when you register and at the end of the free period then 'automatically renew' your subscription. Check to see if there is a tick box that allows you to stop this from happening, or make sure that you cancel your subscription before the renewal period approaches, if you do not wish for a lump sum to suddenly disappear from your bank account! It is also worth signing up to the newsletters and social media platforms of many of the sites, as occasionally you may find offers for periods of free access to certain collections.

FindmyPast Ireland

www.findmypast.ie

FindmyPast Ireland was launched in 2011 as a joint venture between the Dublin-based history and heritage company Eneclann and the Scottish-based technology giant Brightsolid. From the Scottish end it is the latest in a family of genealogical websites, including FindmyPast (**www. findmypast.co.uk**), FindmyPast Australasia (**www.findmypast.com.au**),

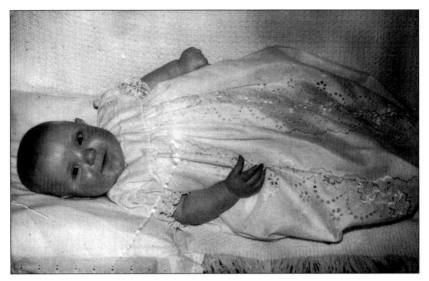

The author's christening in January 1971.

FindmyPast USA (**www.findmypast.com**), Genes Reunited (**www. genesreunited.co.uk**), ScotlandsPeople (**www.scotlandspeople.gov.uk**) and the British Newspaper Archive (**www.britishnewspaperarchive. co.uk**). From an Irish point of view it is of huge significance in that it is trying to offer access to digitised records sourced both by itself and in partnership with bodies such as the National Archives of Ireland.

The British-based FindmyPast website started off as a platform to offer indexes to civil registration records for births, marriages and deaths in England and Wales from 1837 onwards, and later expanded to offer British census records and parish records. As such, it is one of the most significant online platforms to help you get started with British-based research, not just for researching Irish family members who crossed the water, but for UK-wide collections which apply as much to Ireland as to Britain, such as its military holdings. FindmyPast Ireland is a slightly different animal in that it does not offer either civil indexes or much by way of census records. Instead, it is a site which becomes much more useful once you have identified the basics from elsewhere, although it does hold some parish records.

The key holdings of FindmyPast Ireland are arranged in the following categories:

- Vital records (BMDs)
- Censuses & substitutes

FindmyPast Ireland.

- Land & estates
- Courts & legal
- Directories
- Military & rebellion
- Travel & migration

It is now possible through FindmyPast Ireland to take out one of various combined subscriptions that give access to Irish records in conjunction with those from the other FindmyPast websites in the UK, Australasia and the USA. The British site is particularly useful, and includes the following:

- Births, Marriages and Deaths 1538–2006 (England and Wales)
- English and Welsh Censuses 1841–1911, Scottish censuses 1841–1901 (transcriptions only)
- UK Migration Records 1793–1960
- British Army Service Records 1760–1913

Note that if you do take out a subscription, this is automatically renewable after it expires unless you untick the 'Auto-renew my subscription' box in the Personal Details page of the My Account section. If you do not wish to subscribe, there are also several pay-as-you-go options to enable access to the records.

The company also has a regularly updated blog at **http://blog. findmypast.ie**, as well as accounts for Facebook at **www.facebook.com/ findmypast.ie** and Twitter at **@findmypastie**. A tree-building programme is also freely available on the site at **www.findmypast.ie/family-tree**.

Ancestry

www.ancestry.co.uk
Ancestry.co.uk is the UK's platform for the American-based Ancestry.com corporation. In July 2012 the Utah-based company announced plans to set up an international headquarters in Dublin, to deal with its non US-based material, with its world headquarters remaining in Salt Lake City. Although at the time of writing there has been no talk of a separately branded Irish domain for the website, the UK site holds many Irish records on a dedicated subsection of the site at **www.ancestry.co.uk/ cs/uk/ireland**. Among the most useful resources are:

- Irish Civil Registration Birth, Marriage and Death Indexes (1845–1958)
- Births and Baptisms 1620–1911
- Roman Catholic parish records
- Various Irish newspapers, including the *Belfast Newsletter* 1738–1925
- Land records, including Griffith's Valuation and Tithe Applotment books
- Records of the Scots-Irish
- Immigration and travel records
- Royal Irish Constabulary 1816–1921 records
- Photographic collections

There are also many other collections on the main website, including records for Irish-based ancestors, such as the various First World War military collections for the United Kingdom.

Ancestry offers access to its resources either by a monthly or annual subscription, or through a pay-as-you-go model. Bear in mind that, as with FindmyPast, Ancestry memberships are automatically renewable, which means your credit card will be deducted for another term's payment if you do not cancel your membership before your renewal date.

In using certain collections on Ancestry remember to browse the pages *before* the one you land on when you click on a search result, as well as those after, because the page you first arrive at may not necessarily be the first in the particular batch concerning the person of interest. This is particularly true with its First World War service records (see p. 95) and some of its Merchant Navy holdings (see p. 105).

Ancestry also offers free discussion forums and a facility for the hosting of family trees. If you have an Apple- or Android-based computer tablet or phone you can download a free app that allows you to sync your tree on your device to your main Ancestry account on your PC or Mac (see **www.ancestry.co.uk/ancestry-app**). In addition there is an online collaboration tool on the platform called the 'World Archives Project', which allows the company to 'crowd source' collections –in other words to digitise records and have volunteers index them online. This is a worldwide project, which has included Irish collections such as Lord Viscount Morpeth's Testimonial Roll, a recently discovered and highly important substitute for the missing 1841 Irish census (see p. 60). Additional services include DNA testing and print publishing facilities for books, tree charts and posters.

Ancestry has several social media outlets to keep you up to date with new releases, including Twitter at @ancestryUK, Facebook at **www. facebook.com/AncestryUK** and a blog at **http://blogs.ancestry.com/uk**. It is worth keeping an eye out also on the 'View all new records' link on the home page, as this is updated almost daily with additions from its various partner sites across the world. Among the various options available, you can set this to list new Irish sites, those from the United Kingdom, or all countries.

Irish Origins (Origins Network)

www.origins.net

The British-based Origins Network, established in 1997, includes several records areas such as Irish Origins, British Origins and the National Wills Index (containing material for England and Wales).

Irish Origins has many useful resources on its site, arranged in the following categories:

- Census records and census substitutes
- Electoral registers
- Marriage records
- Wills records
- Burial records
- Military, war and rebellion records

- Passenger lists
- Directories
- Places, Maps and Images

Access to the site is gained by either paying for a 72 hours or a monthly pass. Additional options allow you to subscribe to a joint British and Irish package on a similar basis, or through an annual subscription. If you choose a monthly or annual package, your membership will be automatically renewed unless cancelled before your subscription expires.

To keep up to date with developments, you can subscribe to the company's newsletter or its Facebook page at **www.facebook.com/Origins.net**.

Roots Ireland

www.rootsireland.ie
Roots Ireland is the online pay-per-view platform for the transcribed records of the Irish Family History Foundation. The site hosts the largest collection of transcribed Irish parish records online, as well as other records, but it can be quite expensive for what is actually on offer.

The wedding day of Paddy Giles and Pauline Prendergast, in Piltown, Kilkenny, 1960.

Nevertheless, it does cover most of the island, with records sourced from county-based genealogy centres in the north and the south.

The participating counties in the project can be identified by a map on the bottom right of the page, with the counties in green contributing records, those in orange on the point of doing so, and those in red not involved. The records included for each county do vary, however, depending on which projects the respective centres have been working on. This means that while two adjacent counties may both be green on the map, one may only provide Roman Catholic records, while its neighbour may well provide civil records, censuses and Anglican parish records. The site is constantly adding material, so it is always worth returning to look for updates.

You will first need to register to use the site. Once this is done, you can then either perform an Ireland-based search or a more targeted search for a particular county. This can be done by selecting the area of interest using the interactive map on the home page or by accessing the 'County Genealogy Centres' tab on the left column.

Once you have keyed in the search criteria and then pressed return, you will be told how many matches have been found, for which you then need to pay to see the results. Each results page costs one credit and holds up to ten entries, while detailed individual records cost a further twenty-five credits. (In terms of credits, there are discounts available, with various tiers that offer greater savings the more credits you purchase, though the mathematical basis for the lower tiers is bizarre – for example with the lowest option being for the purchase of seventy-three credits. Note also that although you can pay for bulk credits at a substantial discount, you may well then discover that you hit a brick wall with your first search – a case of being all dressed up with credits with nowhere to go.)

Many of the counties which do not participate on Roots Ireland instead have records hosted on another site, **www.irishgenealogy.ie**, which is an Irish Government-sponsored venture that offers access to original images and transcriptions for free. Both sites will be discussed further in Chapter 2.

Emerald Ancestors

www.emeraldancestors.com
For Northern Ireland, Emerald Ancestors is a subscription-based site which provides access to detailed indexes, though not to full transcriptions, of records for civil registration indexes, church registers and other historical sources. It offers a free search facility which provides

partial returns for a query, but you need to subscribe to obtain the complete index details.

There are three tiers of subscription: for a month, six months or a year. If you wish to obtain a full copy of a record identified, the site can provide a look-up service and a facsimile of the original entry, though this can be expensive. The site also offers six ebooks for download, with one book downloadable per month's subscription.

FamilyRelatives

www.FamilyRelatives.com

FamilyRelatives.com is a subscription-based site which offers records predominantly for the UK. It does have some Irish records, such as pre-1858 wills indexes, although much of this content is replicated on other sites. The most useful collection from an Irish perspective is perhaps the overseas British civil registration indexes for events registered with the army, foreign consulates and more, all of which are available to view for free (see p. 36).

The Genealogist

www.TheGenealogist.co.uk

The Genealogist website does not have much by way of Irish holdings, but does carry Griffith's Valuation records and maps (see p. 81), and a few trade directories and land records.

The site offers both subscription and pay-as-you-go options for access, as well as an online family tree-hosting software package called *TreeView*, which can be subscribed to for free at **www.treeview.co.uk**.

Irish Family History

www.irishfamilyresearch.co.uk

Established in 2003, Irish Family History is a subscription-based records platform offering access at two tiers: standard membership, which is free, and full membership at £40 a year. A handful of records sourced from an 1852 *Directory of Belfast & Province of Ulster* are available to access for free, but entry to other databases requires full membership.

As well as its databases, the site does offer a list of members' research interests, useful bibliographies, old photos and postcards, useful contacts for research and more.

Networking and communication

Increasingly there are various sites that allow you to share information and communicate with other researchers or family members across the world. Many free family tree building programmes can be found online, such as Tribal Pages (**www.tribalpages.com**) or Heredis (**www. heredis.com**), while some commercial vendors such as My Heritage (**www.myheritage.com**) and Genes Reunited (**www.genesre united.co.uk**) offer basic tree-building services with many additional features that can be pursued by a subscription. Using such sites you can search in other people's trees for possible connections, and contact them if you find a match with your own.

Various other social networking sites allow you to collaborate by other means apart from a family tree, such as Ancestral Atlas (**www. ancestralatlas.com**), which uses a map as a way for people to locate and establish connections, while Curious Fox (**www.curiousfox.com**) allows connections to be made by village or town names. Lost Cousins (**www.lostcousins.com**) allows connections to be established by the use of census information: pop your relative's 1911 Irish census details in and if someone else does the same, you can establish if your families are related.

Discussion forums can also help, with Rootschat (**www.rootschat.com**) one of the best platforms allowing users to discuss all things genealogical on a county by county basis. Ancestry provides the excellent Rootsweb site (**www.rootsweb.ancestry.com**) which hosts message boards and mailing lists which work in a similar way, while Genealogy Wise (**www.genealogywise.com**) also has many dedicated research groups.

Social networking discussion platforms are also increasingly being used by the day. On Facebook (**www.facebook.com**) you will find many community-based groups, such as the Genealogical Society of Ireland's presence at **www.facebook.com/familyhistory.ie**, while Twitter (**http:// twitter.com**) allows users to 'tweet' short messages of up to 140 characters in length, through what is termed 'micro-blogging'. You will find my address on Twitter as **@chrismpaton**, for example, where I regularly comment on family history developments, as well as providing occasional 'retweets' of other people's announcements from accounts that I follow. I also use the site to provide links to posts on my blog, British GENES (**http://britishgenes.blogspot.co.uk**) on which I carry details of various family history events and developments from across Britain and Ireland, including new records releases online. Another useful genealogy blog is Claire Santry's Irish Genealogy News (**http://irish-genealogy-news.blogspot.ie**).

Irish Lives Remembered magazine is freely available online.

There are several magazines for genealogy, two of which deal specifically with Ireland. *Irish Roots* at **www.irishrootsmedia.com** is a subscription-based quarterly, which offers an e-edition as well as a free online preview. The *Irish Lives Remembered* project at **http://irishlives remembered.com** offers a free monthly magazine of the same name within its magazines section, with each issue downloadable in PDF format. A county-based discussion forum is also available.

In Britain several magazines exist, which occasionally offer Irish content. Of these, *Your Family Tree* (**www.yourfamilytreemag.co.uk**) and *Family Tree* **http://family-tree. co.uk** have e-editions for reading on devices such as iPads, as well as blogs and discussion forums, while *Who Do You Think You Are* magazine (**www.whodoyouthinkyouaremagazine.com**) and *Your Family History* (**www.your-familyhistory.com**) both offer discussion forums and other online content.

Chapter 2

THE VITAL RECORDS

The key records of births, marriages and deaths are known generically as the 'vital records', derived from the Latin word '*vita*', meaning 'life'. The recording of such information is today the responsibility of the state, but prior to the introduction of civil registration in the nineteenth century it was the churches that fulfilled the role through parish registers.

In this chapter I will examine the background to the gathering of such information, as well as the key resources for accessing many of the records online.

Civil registration

The vital records kept by the state contain much information that can help to build up a family tree. Most birth records will provide the name of a child (if decided at the time of registration) and his or her parents, along with details of residence and the father's occupation. A marriage record will name residential and occupational details of the contracting parties, along with the names and details of their fathers (but not their mothers), while records of death will provide the end point for a person's story, though family members will usually only be noted if acting as an informant. The cause of death is also recorded. Websites such as **www.medterms.com/script/main/hp.asp** can help to explain some of the ailments that you may encounter.

Statutory registration in Ireland commenced on 1 April 1845 for marriages performed by the state church, by civil contract or by other religious denominations in the presence of a civil registrar. The Roman Catholic Church objected to this requirement and was therefore exempted. For various reasons pressure soon grew for a more comprehensive system of civil registration, from the need to enforce regulations on smallpox vaccination to issues concerning the employment of Irish labourers in Britain. In January 1864 the system was therefore extended by the state to register all births, marriage and deaths, and the provision for a civil registrar to attend a religious-based marriage ceremony was dropped. Marriages contracted in a registrar's office continued, but from this point onwards religious celebrants of all denominations, including the Roman Catholic Church, also took responsibility for forwarding on the relevant details to the Registrar General. A detailed overview of the history of Irish civil registration, including the various legislative acts passed, is described at **www.groireland.ie/history.htm**.

Records were compiled initially at a local level and then copies transmitted through to the General Register Office (GRO) in Dublin, where they were subsequently indexed. From 1845 to 1877 the indexes were compiled on an annual basis, and then on a quarterly basis from 1878 onwards. The indexing of births changed again in 1903, reverting to an annual system, though this was compensated for by the addition of the mother's maiden name to the index.

Following the Partition of Ireland, the provisions then changed in Ireland. The already established GRO in Dublin continued to administer the Irish Free State, and later the Republic of Ireland. In Northern Ireland a separate GRO was set up in Belfast to cater for registration in Counties Antrim, Down, Armagh, Fermanagh, Tyrone and Londonderry. Birth, marriage and death records for the whole island prior to 1922 remained in Dublin, with copies of registers for the northern counties transmitted to the GRO in Belfast. The net result is that copies of Irish statutory records are now held as follows:

- Civil birth, marriage and death records for the Republic of Ireland's counties can be obtained from 1845 to the present day via the GRO's facility at Roscommon;
- Civil birth, marriage and death records from 1845 to 1921 for Northern Ireland's counties can be obtained from either of the GRO facilities in Roscommon or Belfast; and
- Civil birth, marriage and death records for Northern Ireland from 1922 onwards can *only* be obtained from the General Register Office in Belfast.

Note that copies of records can also be obtained from local civil registration offices in both countries.

To obtain a record from the centralised GROs it is best to first try to identify where and when an event was actually registered, rather than pay for the registrars to perform searches for you, which can be expensive. Although neither country has placed the nationally compiled indexes online yet, they are in fact partially available via two other web-based platforms.

In the 1950s the American-based Church of Jesus Christ of Latter Day Saints microfilmed many, but not all, of the original Irish registers and index volumes to the records. The indexes were later digitised and a database created of the information contained within them, and in January 2009 both were released on the church's FamilySearch website (**www.familysearch.org**). The digitised images were unfortunately removed from the website just a few days later, but the databases remained online.

To locate the database on the FamilySearch site you need to first scroll down to the bottom of the page and look under the 'Browse by Location' heading for a link entitled 'United Kingdom and Ireland'. Once you have clicked on this you will be taken to a new page called 'Historical Record Collections', which will list all of the databases relating to both Britain and Ireland, as well as the Crown dependencies of the Channel Islands and the Isle of Man. To access the Irish collections you can either scroll down the hefty list, which is compiled in alphabetical order, or use the 'Place' filter on the top left of the page: click on 'Ireland' under the 'United Kingdom and Ireland' category.

FamilySearch.

At the time of writing there are actually four separate databases on the site relating to Irish vital records, described as follows:

- Ireland Births and Baptisms, 1620–1881
- Ireland Deaths, 1864–1870
- Ireland Marriages, 1619–1898
- Ireland, Civil Registration Indexes, 1845–1958

The first three collections do contain some entries for civil registration records, but also material compiled from additional sources, mainly parish registers and family histories. These have been extracted from full records that the LDS Church actually holds copies of, and were originally indexed for a huge database called the International Genealogical Index (IGI), but they are now presented as three standalone databases as shown. (Confusingly, however, the IGI itself has since been reinstated onto the FamilySearch website as a 'Legacy' collection at **https://familysearch.org/ search/collection/igi**, so there is now some duplication.) No matter how you access these records, only a small proportion of events registered by the state are included, with births up to 1881 and marriages and deaths predominantly up to 1870, though there is some minor variation across the country. If an ancestor's event does turn up as a transcribed record within one of these it can offer some details, but will still be very incomplete.

Take, for example, the marriage of my three-times-great-grandparents William Watton and Eliza Jane McLaughlin. This is included within the database entitled 'Ireland Marriages 1619–1898', where the transcribed record tells me that the couple wed in Coleraine, County Londonderry, on 7 December 1867. Not only that, but the site also tells me that Elizabeth was aged 20 when she married, and that her father was called Thomas McLaughlin. Completely missing from the transcription, however, is information about where exactly they married in Coleraine (was it at a registry office or a church?), the occupation and abode of Thomas McLaughlin, the name of William's father, his occupation and abode, where William and Eliza themselves resided, or what their occupations were at the time of marriage. What initially appears to be a detailed online entry is in fact woefully short of the full potential of the original record.

So this is where the fourth collection can help – especially if you cannot actually find the record you are looking for within the first three. To access the search screen you need to click on 'Ireland, Civil Registration Indexes, 1845–1958' and you will be taken to a dedicated search page for that collection. An important thing to note is that the title of this record set is actually misleading, for it does not contain records for the whole of Ireland for the period described. The majority of civil records for what is now the Republic are included from 1845–1958 (with a very small number of omissions), but for Northern Ireland the records included are predominantly for the period from 1845 to 1921. A very small number of birth, marriage and death records are available for the north after 1921, although there appears to be neither rhyme nor reason as to how these have been selected.

To locate a particular birth or death record you need to type in the name of the ancestor that you are searching for, a rough date and the place where you believe the death was registered. A slight handicap with the system when it comes to marriage records is that although two parties may be involved, you can still only search for one name at a time. If I return to the example of the marriage for William Watton and Eliza McLaughlin, to look for this marriage I would need to type in 'William' as a first name, 'Watton' as a last name, and then click on the 'Marriage' tag beneath. This then allows me to type in 'Coleraine' and a year range of '1867' to '1867' (for entries in 1867 only!). If I now click on the 'Search' box below, I am taken to a page of results, which in fact lists four separate William Wattons who married in that year. Two are in Strabane, one in Belfast, and only one in Coleraine. The details given for William Watton in Coleraine are as follows:

Name	William Watton
registration district	Coleraine
event type	MARRIAGES
registration quarter and year	1867
estimated birth year	
age (at death)	
mother's maiden name	
film number	101250
volume number	16
page number	609
digital folder number	4179383
image number	00353

There is not a lot to go on here to actually confirm that this is indeed my William, so how do I do so? The answer is that I now need to repeat the search for an Eliza McLaughlin, and then try to match up the details at the bottom of her returned entry with those given for William, namely the volume number and page number.

If I repeat the above search, but type in 'Eliza' and 'McLaughlin' instead, I am again told that there are four possibilities. One appears to be a strong match in Coleraine in 1867, although the name is given as 'Eliza M'Loughlin', while the other three are stated to not be a strong match but of possible interest. If I click on the first entry, the following is returned:

Name	Eliza M'Loughlin
registration district	Coleraine
event type	MARRIAGES
registration quarter and year	1867
estimated birth year	
age (at death)	
mother's maiden name	
film number	101250
volume number	16
page number	609
digital folder number	4179383
image number	00353

This record does not tell me that Eliza married William. The two entries combined, however, do tell me that in 1867 both an 'Eliza M'Loughlin' and a William Watton married in Coleraine, and both happened to have their marriages registered in the exact same marriage register and on the exact same page. In this case I have already established from the earlier database that they did in fact marry, but if I had not found that entry, this find would be such a remarkable coincidence that it would be almost impossible for them to *not* have married!

Performing separate searches can be quite cumbersome to do, particularly if you are looking for popular names such as Mary Murphy and Patrick O'Neill. Fortunately this is where the Ancestry website comes in handy, because it removes a little bit of the pain involved in such a search.

To access Ancestry's Irish civil registration indexes databases I need to visit its Irish page at **www.ancestry.co.uk/cs/uk/ireland**. There is a drop-down menu which states 'All our Irish Collections', and within this is a section entitled 'Birth, marriage and death', and this is where I will find the following datasets:

- Ireland, Civil Registration Births Index, 1864–1958
- Ireland, Civil Registration Deaths Index, 1864–1958
- Ireland, Civil Registration Marriages Index, 1845–1958

The first thing to note about Ancestry's holdings is that they are in fact the exact same databases as those found on FamilySearch. So why visit Ancestry at all, particularly as it is a subscription-based site and FamilySearch is free? The answer is that Ancestry's search screens are actually much better, with the marriage search facility allowing you to do something that FamilySearch does not – it allows you to immediately look for or confirm a spouse once you have identified the first party for a marriage.

Using Ancestry, if I once again wish to carry out a search for William Watton's marriage, I need to select the 'Ireland, Civil Registration Marriages Index, 1845–1958' database and on the search screen type in his name details, the place name 'Coleraine' and the year '1867'. In this

Accessing Ancestry's civil registration indexes from its Irish home page.

instance I am in fact given details of seven gentlemen called William Watton who married in Coleraine – but only one did so in 1867. If I now select the 'View Record' link beside this entry, I am given the following details in return:

Name	William Watton
Date of Registration	1867
Registration district	Coleraine
Volume	16
Page	609 (click to see others on page)
FHL Film Number	101250

There is slightly less information given here than on the FamilySearch site, but the key part is where it states the page number, which is portrayed in blue and underlined as a hyperlink. Beside this in brackets it states 'click to see others on page'. If I do this, the following list is returned:

Catherine Archibald	1867	Coleraine
Mary Anne Boyd	1867	Coleraine
James Hemphill	1867	Coleraine
Benjamin Lighten	1867	Coleraine
Elizabeth M'Loughlin	1867	Coleraine
Mary M'Mullan	1867	Coleraine
Thomas Stewart	1867	Coleraine
William Watton	1867	Coleraine

What this is essentially doing is providing me with the names of all those whose marriages are registered on page 609 of Volume 17 of Coleraine-registered marriages for 1867. In this instance there are four men and four women, and among the latter is 'Eliza M'Loughlin'. This again does not prove that William and Eliza married – this particular William's bride may well have been one of the other three women listed, and the whole thing just a remarkable coincidence – but the odds are that it is the case, and ordering the record from the GRO should hopefully confirm the fact. In some cases searches will reveal only four names recorded on a page, with two men and two women, making the probability even more likely.

Having established when and where an event took place, the next thing to do is to locate the information contained within the original record, by obtaining the certificate itself. There are three main ways in which this can be done.

The first method is the cheapest, but is slightly convoluted because not all of the application can be performed online. The website of the General Register Office in Roscommon, located at **www.groireland.ie**, allows you to access application forms for births, marriages and deaths, as well as adoptions (see p. 33), which you need to download and fill in. These are available in both English and Irish language formats, and can be found on the tab to the side of the page marked 'Apply for Cert'. Once completed, you unfortunately cannot submit them online, but must instead post or fax them through to the GRO.

The GRO charges €10 for a formal legal certificate, which includes a €2 search fee. Fortunately the body also provides a much cheaper alternative in the form of a photocopied extract for research purposes, at a cost of just €6, which includes the €2 fee. The good news is that if you know the full details of the search, including the registration district, volume number and page number (as described above), the GRO will not in fact charge the search fee – effectively meaning a photocopied entry will cost

The GRO Ireland home page.

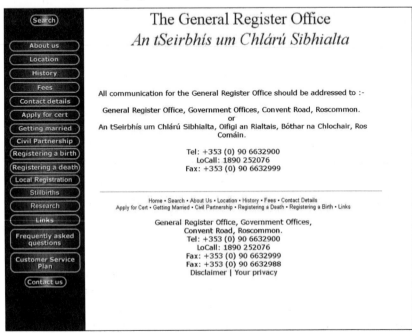

The General Register Office
An tSeirbhís um Chlárú Sibhialta

Search
About us
Location
History
Fees
Contact details
Apply for cert
Getting married
Civil Partnership
Registering a birth
Registering a death
Local Registration
Stillbirths
Research
Links
Frequently asked questions
Customer Service Plan
Contact us

All communication for the General Register Office should be addressed to :-

General Register Office, Government Offices, Convent Road, Roscommon.
or
An tSeirbhís um Chlárú Sibhialta, Oifigí an Rialtais, Bóthar na Chlochair, Ros Comáin.

Tel: +353 (0) 90 6632900
LoCall: 1890 252076
Fax: +353 (0) 90 6632999

Home • Search • About Us • Location • History • Fees • Contact Details
Apply for Cert • Getting Married • Civil Partnership • Registering a Death • Registering a Birth • Links

General Register Office, Government Offices,
Convent Road, Roscommon.
Tel: +353 (0) 90 6632900
LoCall: 1890 252076
Fax: +353 (0) 90 6632999
Fax: +353 (0) 90 6632988
Disclaimer | Your privacy

just €4. Records can be ordered for all of Ireland up to 1921, and for the Republic only from 1922 onwards. Note that the forms do not have boxes asking you to supply the registration district, volume number or page number – but add them anyway! You will be asked to supply your credit card details on the forms also, and once the orders have been processed the records will be posted, usually within a few days. If ordering copies for genealogical purposes only, remember to tick the relevant boxes for this, or you will be sent formal certified extracts at the higher cost.

Many of the records can also be obtained from the Republic of Ireland via the Health Service Executive (HSE). In order to allow access to copies of vital records from any registration office in the country, the Irish Government initiated a project to have them captured in an electronic format. Not all of the records were captured, but at a registration office it is now possible to order any birth record from the whole of Ireland from 1864 to 1921, and for the Republic only from 1922 onwards. For the other records categories there are, however, restrictions. Marriage entries from the whole of Ireland can only be obtained from 1920 to 1921, and for the Republic from 1922 onwards; while death records are only available for the Republic from 1924 onwards. The same records can also be obtained from the HSE at **www.hse.ie/portal/eng/services/Find_a_Service/bdm/ Certificates_ie/**, the good news being that the entire application process can be performed online, including payment. On the downside, you cannot obtain cheaper photocopies for genealogical research purposes only, so records will be formal certified extracts at a cost of €10 each. Note that you will also have to pay an extra Euro for postage, which the GRO does not charge through its service. This site's application forms also do not ask for registration district, volume or page number, but if you have the details, put them in.

The third option for certificates is to obtain them from the GRO in Belfast, which can produce copies of all marriages from 1845 onwards for the six counties of Northern Ireland, as well as births and deaths for the north from 1864 onwards. In recent years I have always avoided using this method for pre-1922 events, however, for the simple reason of cost – the GRO in Belfast charges a whopping £15 plus postage, with no cheaper option of a simple photocopy. As copies of the same records can be obtained from Roscommon for just €4 each – a quarter of the price – it has been a no-brainer in terms of where to go. For post-1921 events, however, there is no alternative but to order records online from Belfast.

The current situation is that you can make an order online through the GRONI site via **www.nidirect.gov.uk/gro**. You can elect to do the whole process electronically online and pay by credit or debit card, or download an application form and post your application with a cheque or postal order. It is worth noting that for entries obtained for the north prior to 1922, the volume number and page number obtained from Ancestry or FamilySearch will not be of much use, as the records are indexed separately by the Belfast-based GRO. However, the details of the registration district, and the year and quarter, will certainly still help.

The process is expensive, but a minor miracle is about to happen for those with Northern Irish ancestry, inspired by a system already available in Scotland. In Scotland, indexes to civil registered births, marriages and deaths from 1855 to the present day have been available online for a decade via a pay-per-view website called ScotlandsPeople (**www.scotlands people.gov.uk**). For just £7 you can purchase thirty credits for use on the site, with which you can search the records, with each detailed index entry costing one credit to view. Digitised images from many of the actual register records themselves are also available, for a further five credits, subject to a series of closure periods – for births older than a hundred years, marriages over seventy-five years, and deaths over fifty years ago. More recent records need to be ordered as certified extracts from the National Records of Scotland, which incorporates the Scottish GRO.

The truly wonderful news is that a similar set-up for Northern Ireland, directly inspired by the Scottish example, is currently under preparation. When it goes online, it should be nothing short of a revolutionary development for northern-based research.

Other civil records sources

Several other sites have also indexed at least some of the civil registration records. Jane Lyon's From Ireland site at **www.from-ireland.net** has indexes to births, marriages and deaths, though Jane does point out that the references are entirely random, and that 'for some surnames all references over a period of years have been taken'.

County Waterford's library also hosts free to access indexes for all death records from 1 January 1864 to 31 December 1901 at **www.water fordcountylibrary.ie/en/familyhistory/deathregisters**. Birth and marriage records are not indexed, however.

Some online vendors have transcribed copies of civil records incorporated within their databases, or have created their own indexes. The coverage on Roots Ireland (see p. 17) varies from county to county, but its exact holdings can be determined through the 'Online Sources' tab on the left of the screen, and the sub-heading 'List of Sources'. For some counties there are no entries at all, but for those where there are, note that neither the index entries nor the records transcriptions appear to include the volume numbers and page numbers from the original GRO sources, although the registration districts are listed. The information provided should still be enough to allow you to order the records from the respective GRO if required. At the time of writing, civil records are included for counties Armagh, Derry, Donegal, Galway (east), Kilkenny, Leitrim, Limerick, Mayo, Monaghan (Dawsongrove marriages only), Roscommon and Tipperary. The coverage dates vary, with some counties holding records up to 1900 only, for example, and others up to 1921.

Emerald Ancestors (p. 18) includes civil records within its vital records entries, with births for the six counties of Northern Ireland from 1864 to 1876 and marriages from 1845 to 1920, but no civil death records. It is not possible to determine from a free search which records are sourced from parish records and which are from civil registration. Once registered the returned index entries do usually make it clear, but again they do not contain the source information from the GRO, just some limited details. There should still be enough information to order a certificate from the GRO, or you can pay for a full transcript.

Adoption
Adoption was legalised in Northern Ireland in 1929 and in the Republic of Ireland from 1953.

The General Register Office for Northern Ireland has a detailed adoption guide for those wishing to trace birth parents, which includes information on how to sign up to join the Adoption Contact Register. From **www.nidirect.gov.uk/gro** click on the 'Adoption (Parents section)' link, and then go to the last option on the next page, entitled 'Tracing and contacting birth relatives and adopted adults'. Adoptees older than 18 have a right to obtain their original birth certificate and the site discusses the various methods for doing so, with different rules for those born before or after 1987 – online application forms for both are also available.

The GRO in Roscommon offers online application forms at **www.groireland.ie/apply_for_a_cert.htm** for those wishing to obtain a certified copy of an entry in the Adopted Children Register. For a guide on how to trace birth parents you will need to consult the Health Service Executive site at **www.hse.ie/eng**. Type in 'Tracing Services' in the search box at the top right of the screen for the relevant guide, which also includes details of various support services you may require.

Indexes in Britain
Given Ireland's close proximity to Britain, it is entirely possible that your Irish ancestors may have spent time working or living across the water.

Your wee granny from Sligo may actually be your wee granny from Portsmouth, born to Irish parents in England, while other ancestors may have married in Britain and possibly even died there. Many of the gaps within Irish records can sometimes be plugged through an exploration of their British equivalents.

Civil registration first commenced in England and Wales in July 1837, with Scotland not following suit until January 1855. When looking for records in Britain it is worth bearing in mind that civil registration was in fact established under two separate legal systems, namely English Law and Scots Law. The level of information returned for English and Welsh records is virtually the same as that returned for Irish records: so, for example, in a birth record both parents will be named, whereas in a marriage record only the fathers of a couple are named, and in death records, no parental information is given at all (unless the parent was an informant). In Scotland, however, virtually every birth, marriage and death record will record the names of both parents, including the mother's maiden name, while Scottish birth records also uniquely note the date and place where a child's parents were married (except from 1856 to 1860).

As an example of how useful the British records can be, for many years I was unaware that a County Londonderry-born great-grandfather of mine, Robert Currie, who migrated to Glasgow in the 1890s, in fact had a brother called Jackson Currie, who had travelled to Scotland before him. Robert's parents had married in Ireland in 1853, but with no civil birth records recorded in the country until 1864, I had only previously found siblings for him that were born after this year. When I was later alerted to the possibility of Jackson being a brother, I immediately located his death record in Scotland via the ScotlandsPeople website. This not only listed an age indicating a possible birth in 1855, which was later corroborated by further work with the Scottish censuses, but also that he shared the same parents as Robert. Just for good measure, my great-grandfather turned out to be the informant to the registrar in Glasgow for Jackson's eventual death. For more on ScotlandsPeople, and how to access Scottish civil records, see p. 32.

Unlike the Irish system, records for England and Wales were compiled in quarterly returns consistently from 1837 to 1983, and thereafter on an annual basis. There are several websites hosting the relevant indexes up to 2006. The FreeBMD website at **www.freebmd.org.uk** is a volunteer project which does what it says on the tin, with volunteers transcribing the indexes and placing them online for free. For the nineteenth century the database is virtually complete, while a significant amount of records for the twentieth century are already uploaded. Several commercial vendors also provide access, including Ancestry, FindmyPast.co.uk, The Genealogist and FamilyRelatives. Once you have found the correct index reference number you can order a copy of the required record from the General Register Office in Southport, via **www.gro.gov.uk/gro/content/ certificates/default.asp**.

Overseas British records

With Ireland's membership of the UK there is also another major source for civil records detailing Irish folk, and that is the records held by the General Register Office in Southport for events registered overseas. There are several such collections, including military chaplaincy services (1796–1880), regimental birth registers (1761–1924), Army Returns and Service Department Registrations (1880–1965), consular and High Commission services, registers of shipping and seamen, and much more. A full detailed guide to the various collections is available on the FindmyPast UK website at **www.findmypast.co.uk/help-and-advice/ knowledge-base/overseas-military/records**.

These records not only are available in many cases for periods prior to the establishment of domestic-based Irish and British civil registration, but in some cases can actually be more detailed. The following case study gives an example of their worth, and shows how a search beyond the confines of Ireland's borders can often reap dividends.

From the 1901 and 1911 Irish censuses (see p. 62) I discovered that my great-great-grandmother Florence Graham, née Halliday, was not from Belfast as I had at first believed, but had in fact been born on the island of Gibraltar in approximately 1863. The census showed that although Florence and her husband Edwin had many children born in Ireland, their eldest son Edwin had in fact been born in Scotland. Using the ScotlandsPeople site (see p. 32) I consulted his birth record and established that Florence's full name was Florence Teresa Halliday, and that she and her husband had in fact married in Barrow-in-Furness in England on 27 June 1881. From this I was then able to locate their marriage certificate from the English GRO at Southport, which gave me details about Florence's father: a deceased military bandmaster called Alexander William Halliday.

Knowing that Florence was born in Gibraltar, I then tried to locate her birth record. The indexes to the British overseas events are located on three main sites. The Genealogist has a searchable database entitled 'Overseas BMDs', where you can search each of the collections individually, while FindmyPast UK also hosts the records, although these are fully integrated into the site's main BMD indexes. If you do not wish to take out a subscription to these, however, the FamilyRelatives site (p. 19) has the index records available to browse in its 'Free' section, where it is also possible to consult each collection individually. From these indexes I soon located an entry that seemed to fit, in the 'GRO Regimental Birth Indices' collection. The details given were as follows:

Name	Halliday, Florence T.
Place	Gibraltar
Year	1863
Regt.	2nd
Volume	996
Page	11

To order such an overseas certificate online you need to use the English GRO website at **www.gro.gov.uk/gro/content/certificates/default.asp**. Rather than use the standard application screen for births, marriages and deaths under 'Certificate Types', you need to scroll down the page further

British Overseas Records indexes are available for free on FamilyRelatives.

to the subheading 'For overseas events which were registered with the British authorities', and place your order here.

In this case, I obtained the certificate, which presented the following information:

Regt	2nd Battalion 2nd Regiment of Foot
Date of birth	7 Sept 1863
Place of baptism	Gibraltar
Date of baptism	11 Oct 1863
Christian name	Florence Teresa
Parents names	Alexander Halliday, Teresa
Rank of father	Corpl
Name of Chaplain	Revd T. Gardiner C. F.

Using the same indexes I was now able to establish that Florence's parents had married overseas prior to her birth, the wedding having occurred on the island of Corfu in 1862. In this case the marriage was discovered in a separate collection, the 'GRO Ionian Islands Civil Register of Marriage' indexes. Again, note the information offered compared to an Irish birth certificate:

Date	1862 June 27
Names	Alexander William Halliday, bachelor, Corporal 2/2 Regt (Queens), full age, dwelling in Corfu
	Teresa Mooney, spinster, full age, dwelling in Corfu
Parents	William Alexander and Martha Ann Halliday
	Thomas and Mary Ann Mooney
Celebrated	Garrison Church
Rite	Church of England
Witnesses	Sydney Cluck M.A. Chaplain to the Forces
	James Crabtree
	Catherine Elizabeth Johnson
Entry date	1862 June 27

I continued the research and discovered the family had later been posted to Bermuda, where they had a son called Alexander, and that Alexander senior had subsequently died there in 1866. The surviving family members relocated to Ireland, and it was not until the 1901 census that I was once again able to pick up Florence's mother Teresa in the records (she had since remarried and again been widowed), living with her son Alexander in Dublin. The record in fact noted that Teresa was originally from the city of Dublin, confirming an Irish connection after all – albeit at the end of an international trail from Belfast to Dublin, taking in Scotland, England, Gibraltar, Corfu and Bermuda along the way! Teresa eventually died in Dublin in 1919 and was buried at Glasnevin Cemetery (see p. 48).

Matheson's Reports

It can be particularly galling when a place of origin is simply identified in an overseas-based census record as 'Ireland'. If you have no idea where on the island your ancestors may have come from, there are a couple of online resources that may be of assistance with your research in trying to establish a starting point. Thanks to the efforts of a former Irish Registrar General, Sir Robert Edwin Matheson, there is a useful resource from 1894 entitled *Special Report on Surnames in Ireland with Notes as to Numerical Strength, Derivation, Ethnology and Distribution* that might be able to narrow down the options. Matheson took the data from the 1890 birth registers to compile a statistical report detailing surname distributions across the island of Ireland. This work has since been digitised and made available online via the Internet Archive at **http://archive.org/details/cu31924029805540**. If you wish to do a spot-check on the frequency of a particular surname, there is also a free to access database online at **www.ancestryireland.com/database.php?filename=db_mathesons**, employing Matheson's data. This predominantly breaks down results by province, though a short explanation with each surname returned does list the principal counties where it will be found.

A follow-up book by Matheson from 1901, entitled *Varieties and Synonymes of Surnames and Christian Names in Ireland: for the guidance of registration officers and the public in searching the indexes of births, deaths, and marriages*, can also be found online at **http://archive.org/details/varietiessynonym00math**. This is particularly useful for identifying variants of surnames which may have been used when registering events – particularly for those which have been translated from Irish to English, with some families registering events under different names at different times.

Incidentally, surname distributions can also be worked out using other resources such as the 1901 and 1911 census databases (see p. 62), where you can note the frequency of occurrences by individual counties in each census year. Another resource worth consulting is the Irish Origenes site at **www.irishorigenes.com**, which has a map-based database showing the frequency of 4,500 surnames found across the island, as recorded in the 1911 census.

Parish registers

Prior to the advent of civil registration in both 1845 and 1864, the main records for establishing births, marriages and deaths are those of the various church denominations. Bear in mind that although the Roman Catholic Church was (and remains) by far the largest denomination on the island, the Anglican-based Church of Ireland was in fact the country's established church up to 1869, and in many ways acted as a state department. As such, you may well find that a record for a person from a non-Anglican denomination is recorded in an Anglican register. Catholicism was heavily discriminated against until the advent of the Catholic Relief Act in 1829, and one unfortunate consequence is that most Catholic parishes have little by way of coverage prior to the early nineteenth century. On the other hand, while a significant proportion of Church of Ireland records were destroyed by fire in 1922, the Roman Catholic registers largely survived, being held in local custody.

If your ancestor was Catholic in origin, it is relatively easy to note which records exist, and where to access copies. The National Library of Ireland has an online guide at **www.nli.ie/en/parish-register.aspx** detailing the parish records it holds on microfilm, which mostly go up to 1880, but in some cases to 1900. In due course the institution hopes to digitise these and make them available online. The *Irish Times*-hosted Irish Ancestors site has a more comprehensive guide to Roman Catholic records online at **www.irishtimes.com/ancestor/browse/counties/rcmaps/**. This has an interactive map that allows you to first select a county of interest, and then a Catholic parish, to identify where records may be held. Once the parish of interest is found, it provides a summary of areas where copies of the required material are held, microfilm call numbers and links to online collections. If I select the parish of Drumraney in County Westmeath, for example, I can discover that records from 1834 to 1880 are held on microfilm at both the National Library of Ireland and at the LDS Church's Family History Library, but that transcripts have also been made available online at the Roots Ireland website by Dún na Sí Heritage and Genealogical Centre. The entry also tells me that there is an extra twenty years' worth of records on this website, with coverage in fact extending here from 1834 to 1900.

The Public Record Office of Northern Ireland has microfilm copies of church records as well, and provides an equally useful document online to help find them. The 337-page *A Guide to Church Records* at **www.proni.gov.uk/guide_to_church_records.pdf** itemises the records held at the archive from across the entire province of Ulster (including records from Donegal, Monaghan and Cavan), as well as some holdings for parishes in Louth. The records come from many different denominations, and are listed in alphabetical order. If the records for a particular church are not at PRONI, the institution has tried to list where they can be located instead. PRONI also has a separate page at **www.proni.gov.uk/index_to_roman_catholic_records-6.pdf** listing Roman Catholic parish registers up to 1880 held on microfilm for the nine counties of Ulster (this document was compiled in 2008).

If I look up my home town of Carrickfergus in the first document, I discover that PRONI holds records for several denominations within the historic borough, including Baptist, Congregational, Church of Ireland, Methodist, Presbyterian and Roman Catholic. However, Carrickfergus

St Nicholas Church in Carrickfergus.

also provides a good example of how tragic the coverage of parish records can be. The town's Anglican church of St Nicholas, built by the Normans in 1182, has the oldest surviving vital records, but they exist from 1740 only. Although the first Irish-based presbytery was formed in the town by chaplains accompanying a Scottish Covenanting army in 1642, the earliest baptism and marriage records for the town's first Presbyterian church survive from 1823. This is just five years earlier than the town's Roman Catholic records, extant from 1828.

Some Church of Ireland parish records are also held in Dublin at the Representative Church Body Library (RCBL), which has a website at **http://ireland.anglican.org/about/42**. A detailed guide on these can be found at **www.ireland.anglican.org/cmsfiles/pdf/AboutUs/library/parregs.pdf**, with some of the records now also appearing online (see below), while a database identifying the existence of vestry records held at the RCBL is at **www.progenealogists.com/ireland/churchireland.asp**. Additional catalogues describing related holdings are available at **http://ireland.anglican.org/about/105**. The National Archives of Ireland has a similar listing of Church of Ireland records held on microfilm at **www.nationalarchives.ie/PDF/CofIMicrofilms.pdf**, and also offers a map of the church's dioceses at **www.nationalarchives.ie/genealogy/churchmap.html**. An unusual source held by the facility that might help with obtaining information from many of the Anglican registers which were lost is a series of thirteen volumes compiled from pension applications after 1908, where parish records were used to provide proof of age for those applying, along with extracts from the 1841 and 1851 censuses (see p. 67). A useful 29-page document listing the parishes for which such surrogate material exists is located at **www.nationalarchives.ie/PDF/CofIReplacements.pdf**. The records can be very hit and miss, however, often naming only one person from a particular parish.

There are, of course, many websites offering access to parish records holdings of all faiths, some for free and some on a commercial basis. In terms of free access, by far the most brilliant source online is the Irish Genealogy website at **www.irishgenealogy.ie**, a site both sponsored and hosted by the Irish Government's Department of Arts, Heritage and the Gaeltacht. It offers some three million church records for the period prior to 1900 for several areas in Ireland, including Carlow (Anglican), Cork and Ross (Catholic, excludes Cork City), Dublin City (Anglican, Catholic and some Presbyterian) and Kerry (Anglican and Catholic). There are no records online at the time of writing for Monaghan, but some Catholic records are promised for the county in due course. With the exception of three parishes in Dublin, there are no Roman Catholic burial records on the site, so you should check the Anglican burial records for the equivalent areas of interest (if available).

The site's records can be searched by accessing the 'Search Church Records' tab at the top. From the returned screen you can look for information by person, location and date, or simply browse the holdings. The actual records are presented both as transcripts and as digitised scans from the original registers. You can further narrow down searches to particular churches and areas using the filters on the left-hand side of the screen showing the search returns. Before your search do check the 'Latest Updates' section on the home page first, as from here you can access detailed parish listings for each area represented, noting the types of records available and the years of coverage. A direct link is available at **http://irishgenealogy.ie/record_list.html**. This could save a lot of effort, before you spend ages trying to find a record that may not actually be there!

Unfortunately at the time of writing, plans to expand the site's offerings appear to be on hold. As a consequence, the Representative Church Body Library (see p. 41), which supplied the Anglican records for the project, has decided to add further records online via its Anglican Records Project at **http://ireland.anglican.org/about/151**, with the first release being for Delgany (Glendalough) in County Wicklow.

Roots Ireland (see p. 17) has an extensive range of parish records on its website, though the coverage varies between counties. To establish what is available for each region visit the site's 'Online Sources' section via a button on the left side of the home page and then choose the 'List Sources' option. From here you can then use the drop-down menu to select the county of interest. The holdings of various denominations are grouped together in individual sections, making it easy to readily see what is available.

It is worth bearing in mind that records may not necessarily always be found in the place where you think they should be, as the documents being worked on by the transcribers may come from repositories beyond the county in question. A good example on the Roots Ireland site lies with records for one of my wife's ancestral towns, Carrick-on-Suir, in County Tipperary. The town is located to the south-west of Tipperary, so naturally enough there are records to be found on the South Tipperary page, specifically Roman Catholic baptismal records from 1784 to 1880 and marriage records from 1788 to 1880. However, as the town's name suggests, Carrick lies on the River Suir. On the other side of this waterway is another part of the town, Carrickbeg, which is actually in County Waterford! If I check the holdings for the Waterford page on

Roots Ireland, not only do I find Roman Catholic baptisms for Carrick-on-Suir listed for the year 1788 and for Carrickbeg in 1842, but also Roman Catholic marriages for Carrick-on-Suir from 1786 to 1983 and Carrickbeg from 1807 to 1965! It doesn't end there, for the page also has Church of Ireland marriage records for Carrick-on-Suir from 1769 to 1926, a denomination completely missing from the South Tipperary site.

It used to be the case on Roots Ireland that you could search for the names of children to a named couple by both parish and religious denomination (or civil registration district for civil records) and year range. Sadly this very useful facility was removed from the site in early 2012. It is still possible to perform a more limited parent search, however, but now only by county and year range. Simply select the type of record you wish to search for, and then type in the father's and mother's names, and then click 'Search' (you only need to type in the surnames for this if you are having problems with first name variants). You will be told how many results are available, but will now have to pay one credit to see the basic returns (per page of returns).

If you know the name of a child and his or her parents, but are unsure when he or she was born, you can type in both parents' names and the child's first name, and narrow it down to the parish and denomination. By typing in a year and playing with the range, you will be able to hone it down to the correct year at no cost at all. In fact, the search criteria are quite flexible – in a baptismal or birth search, for example, if you don't know the name of a child's parents, you can type in the child's first name and the father's surname to perform a search within a parish. If you get a hit, you can then try inputting one letter at a time as a search term for the start of the father's first name; once found, then try to work out what the second letter is, and then the third etc., until you establish the full name. Despite the limitations the site has imposed, by being a bit creative with how you perform searches you can in fact still achieve a great deal more than may at first seem possible.

Elsewhere, Emerald Ancestors (p. 18) includes parish records that have been indexed, with baptisms from as early as 1796 and marriages from 1823 for the Northern Irish counties. There is unfortunately no source area on the site to help you determine whether a parish of interest to you is included. This means that unless you have a subscription, you cannot tell at which church a baptism or marriage occurred. The news section of the site does list the names of some parishes for which records have been added, as and when they were uploaded, though only a small number are described.

FindmyPast Ireland offers some parish-based baptismal and marriage records of various denominations, although nothing like the amount on its British counterpart. At the time of writing the following collections were available:

- Marriage Licence Bonds: Diocese of Cloyne 1630–1800
- Farrar's Index to Irish Marriages 1771–1812 (extracted from the *Hibernian* magazine)
- Register of Derry Cathedral, 1642–1703
- Registers of the French Non-Conformist Churches Dublin 1701–1831
- The Parish Register Society of Dublin, The Registers of St Patrick, Dublin, 1677–1800, 1907
- Thomas Philip Le Fanu, Registers of the French Church of Portarlington, Ireland, 1694–1816
- Clonfert Marriage Bonds 1663–1857
- Raphoe Marriage Bonds 1710–55 and 1817–30

Ancestry's offerings are likewise fairly hit and miss. Its largest collections are those comprising eighteenth- and nineteenth-century Roman Catholic

The Roman Catholic Church of Assumption in Piltown, Co. Kilkenny, where the author was married in 2000.

records, with baptisms from 1742 to 1881 (275,298 records), marriages and banns from 1742 to 1884 (128,618 records) and parish deaths from 1756 to 1881 (29,644 records). These actually contain a relatively small amount of entries when you consider the size of the whole population, but there is coverage for various regions, with the largest collections for Counties Meath, Roscommon and Louth. Several of the large FamilySearch databases are also available on the site.

Additional resources include *Farrar's Index to Irish Marriages* (titled by Ancestry as the 'Index to Irish Marriages, 1771–1812' collection), and an 'Irish Records Extraction Database' with 100,000 names derived from various resources, covering the period 1600–1874. Quite what is contained in this is not detailed. Other collections of interest on the site include:

- Dublin, Ireland, Probate Record and Marriage Licence Index, 1270–1858
- The registers of the Church of St Michan, Dublin
- The register of the parish of St Peter and St Kevin, Dublin
- Knocktemple Old Cemetery Inscriptions, County Cavan, Ireland
- The registers of St John the Evangelist, Dublin: 1619–1699
- The registers of St Catherine, Dublin, 1636–1715
- Louth, Ireland, Extracted Parish Records

A search through the gateway sites listed on p. 2 will provide some additional resources for parish record transcriptions. Among the best are the free to access Irish Genealogy Project Archives at **www.igp-web.com/IGPArchives/index.htm**, which contains masses of volunteer transcripts of registers from across Ireland, while additional material for Roscommon, Clare and Galway can also be found at A Little Bit of Ireland, at **http://celticcousins.net/ireland**. Images of many churches across the island can be found online at **www.churches-uk-ireland.org/county_index.html**.

In terms of the history of various ecclesiastical jurisdictions and subjects, including a history of Quakers and the 1932 Eucharistic Congress, the Ask About Ireland portal has several digitised ebooks that may be of interest at **http://tinyurl.com/irelandchurchhistory**. A list of Quaker wills is online at **www.failteromhat.com/quaker/quakerindex.htm**, and an interesting article by Kenneth L. Carroll about the settlement of Quaker weavers in Newport from 1720 to 1740 in the *Journal of the Friends' Historical Society* (1976, vol. 54) is well worth reading at **www.reocities.com/Heartland/Park/7461/quakerweavers.pdf**.

If your ancestors were French Huguenots, FindmyPast Ireland has some records for the French Church of Portarlington from 1694 to 1816, as well as records for Dublin-based congregations at Peter Street and Lucy Lane from 1701 to 1831. For Methodist research, the Methodist Church of Ireland has a genealogy advice page at **www.irish methodist.org/about/genealogy.php**. Additional details on some useful Methodist resources can also be found at **http://irishmethodistgenealogy. wordpress.com/3-booksearch/**.

Those with Jewish ancestry in Ireland should consult the Irish Jewish Genealogical Society at **www.irishjewishroots.com,** as well as the Knowles Collection database for the British Isles – this is located in the 'Jewish Families' section of FamilySearch's Community Trees site at **http://histfam.familysearch.org**.

For Orange Order research, the Grand Orange Lodge of Ireland has an online presence at **www.grandorangelodge.co.uk**. This provides various articles on its history, as well as information on its archives at Schomberg House in Belfast, which includes many lodge books dating back to 1796. The 'Links' page also provides connections to its equivalents in Canada, England, Scotland and the United States.

Burials

In the north, the most impressive burial records site is a free to access database placed online by Belfast City Council at **www.belfastcity.gov.uk/ burialrecords**. This contains details of burials from the city's three main cemeteries still under the council's control, namely Belfast City Cemetery from 1869 to the present day (including the Jewish, Public and Glenalina extensions), Roselawn Cemetery from 1954 onwards, and Dundonald Cemetery from 1905. The database does not carry records for Balmoral Cemetery, Clifton Street Graveyard, Friar's Bush Graveyard, Knock Burial Ground or Shankill Graveyard.

The basic search fields are found at the bottom of the page and are limited to forename, surname and year. Once a search is performed the initial information provided includes the deceased's name, date of death, date of burial and the cemetery of interment. The final columns provide two further options, the first being a link within each entry allowing you to 'View Details', the second being one that is not returned for all entries, but which when it does states 'Add to basket: £1.50'. If more than one record with a candidate's name is held, then the results are displayed in groups of five at a time.

If I do a search for my great-great-grandmother Florence Graham, who died in 1911, I am initially told that there are two people who died that

Roselawn Cemetery in Belfast.

year with the name. One was aged 5 months, the other 48 years. By clicking on 'View Details' for the second, I get the following:

Name of deceased:	Mrs Florence Graham
Last place of residence:	67 Duncairn Gardens
Age:	48 Years
Sex:	
Date of death:	18 September 1911
Date of burial:	20 September 1911
Cemetery:	City Cemetery
Grave section and number:	B 513
Burial type:	Earth Burial

The cemetery name, along with details for the grave section and number, are underlined and in blue, meaning that they are clickable hyperlinks. Clicking on 'City Cemetery' takes me to a separate page providing information on the history of the cemetery, as well as some images and details of its location. The 'Grave section and number' link, however, is much more useful for research, in that it takes you to a new page listing all of those who have been buried within the same lair. In this case the site reveals that there were in fact six people buried in the same plot, all clearly named as members of the same Graham family. This ability to search the lair number was introduced in early 2012; if you used the site prior to this, it is worth going back for another look.

The council has now also added a pay-per-view feature to allow users to download the original burial records themselves. By adding a record of interest to the basket, and paying £1.50, even more information can be accessed. Purchasing Florence's record of burial reveals that the funeral was expected to take place after 11am on the day of burial, the lair owner was Edwin Graham (her husband), her religion was 'Epis' (Episcopalian), the cause of her death was chronic nephritis, and the fee for burial was 7s 6d. Compared to an equivalent death record, it is immediately obvious that not only does this burial record contain more information, it is also considerably cheaper.

Another useful research tool for areas further afield in the north is the History from Headstones project at **www.historyfromheadstones.com**. This is a pay-per-view site with some 50,000 memorial inscriptions from across Northern Ireland. Each look-up costs a pricey £4, but if you sign up to membership of the Ulster Historical Foundation you can get unlimited access. An interactive map identifies which cemeteries are included at **www.historyfromheadstones.com/index.php?id=686**.

In the Republic, Dublin's Glasnevin Trust provides an online pay-per-view database at **www.glasnevintrust.ie/genealogy/** offering access to 1.5 million records from Dardistown, Newlands Cross, Palmerstown and Goldenbridge cemeteries, as well as Glasnevin and Newlands Cross crematoria. The site allows you to perform a free basic search, where you can type in the first and last names of a person you are interested in, and the year of burial. If I was to search for the burial of my three-times-great-grandmother Teresa Burns (mother of Florence Graham in the Belfast example), I would type in the name and the year of death, which in this case is 1919. The following basic information is then returned in a series of columns:

Surname:	Burns
First Name:	Teresa
Address:	Dublin
Location:	Glasnevin
D.O.D.	1919
Ceremony:	Burial
Age:	83
Sex	F

The last two columns also provide more information that can inform my choice of how to proceed. The first is headed with a simple question mark, which in this case is ticked – this means that there are additional people buried in the same lair, though a cautionary note does explain that 'it is possible they may have had no relationship to one another nor to the grave owner'. The second and last column offers three Purchase options: 'Standard', 'Extended' and 'Show Entry Image'. The Standard option costs three credits (with each credit costing a Euro) and allows me to see the entry for Teresa only. The extended option, at eight credits cost, includes all those named in the same lair. If there are digitised images from the original burial register available ('Book Extracts'), the last option allows me to see this for an additional two credits.

If in this case I elect to see all of those in the lair via the Extended option, upon payment of the fee I now obtain additional information on Teresa. The record confirms that I have the right Teresa Burns, as it states her known Dublin address of 3 Synnot Row. It also confirms the exact date of death as 16 May 1919 and gives the lair number to locate her, as well as the fact that she is buried in the St Bridget's section of the cemetery. It transpired that there was only one other person in the grave, a Thomas Hogg, but, as the site warned, he appears to have had no connection to the family.

Note that if a search term returns many possibilities, or none at all, at the bottom of the returns page you can use an 'Advanced Search' facility to narrow down or broaden your options. For both the first name and last name you can leave it blank or use the 'Contains' filter, you can include some details from an address that you might have, and you can add a plus or minus range of one or three years to the year you select. It's irritatingly fiddly, but it may help. Another irritation with the site is the awkward method for registration. In order to register, you have to provide a mobile phone number, to which the system then sends a password for you to sign in.

Bear in mind also that for Dublin there is another site offering records for Glasnevin Cemetery itself, and that is the Irish Genealogy Project Archives at **www.igp-web.com/IGPArchives/index.htm**. This is free to access and not only contains headstone photographs and transcriptions from Glasnevin, but also for Dublin's Deansgrange and Mount Jerome burial grounds, as well as other areas around the country via its 'Cemetery Records' and 'Headstones' categories. Before leaving the capital, another useful online resource is the Dublin Graveyards Directory from Dublin City Library and Archive, which can be found at **http://dublinheritage.ie/graveyards**. This is a handy ready-reckoner

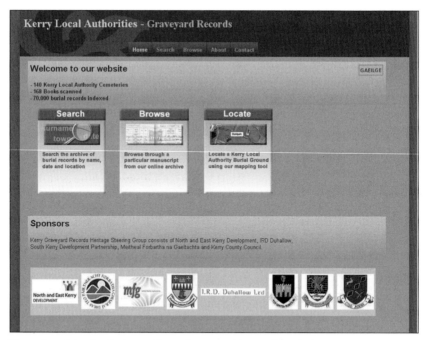

Kerry Local Authority's excellent Graveyard Records website.

that can help you to locate additional graveyards and any relevant burial records, including details of any publications containing transcriptions.

The wonderful Kerry Local Authorities Graveyards Records site at **www.kerrylaburials.ie/en/Index.aspx** holds some 70,000 records from 140 cemeteries in the county, in the form of 168 digitised and free to access burial registers books. It is fully searchable by cemetery, townland or street, surname, forename and date range. The same collection is incidentally also searchable on the Ancestry website, though once you find a name it simply steers you to the Kerry site to see the records. A handy Google map at **http://atomik.kerrycoco.ie/map_pages/map_ burial_grounds.htm** also plots where the individual cemeteries are located.

A similar local authority-sponsored digitisation project is the Mount St Lawrence Burial Ground Registers 1855–2008 collection from Limerick Archives, located at **http://limerick.ie/Archives/MountStLawrence BurialGroundRegisters1855-2008/**. Here you will find four burial registers from 1855 to 2008, although this is not searchable and needs to be browsed. You will need to download a DjVu viewer to browse the records if your computer does not have this. Although burial register images for Waterford are not online, there is a useful 'Grave Memorial Database' from Waterford County Council Library Service at **www.waterfordcountylibrary.ie/en/familyhistory/gravememorials/**.

The Irish Graveyards Surveyors site at **www.irishgraveyards.ie** has an extensive and growing free to access database of burials in many graveyards north and south, though the largest coverage is for Counties Donegal, Galway and Mayo. The site offers an interactive map to help you locate the graveyard of interest, with red dots indicating burial grounds already surveyed and blue dots those that have been commissioned. Alternatively the search page at **www.irishgraveyards.ie/search_page.php** also lists the sites and provides an interface to help you locate individual burials. The databases can be searched by name, or you can browse photographs of all the headstones by the relevant graveyard. Individual lair numbers are also provided, and graveyard maps indicating where each burial is located. For sites that have been surveyed there are also photographs provided of the churches in question and links to any relevant parish home pages.

Additional all-Ireland repositories holding burials material include From Ireland at **www.from-ireland.net** with some 19,200 monumental inscriptions, while the Cemetery Records Online site carries many useful transcribed records. Its southern Irish holdings are available at **www.interment.net/ireland/index.htm**, with northern holdings accessible at **www.interment.net/uk/nire/index.htm**. A community-based initiative is Historic Graves at **http://historicgraves.ie,** which is a volunteer-based project surveying graveyards across the Republic. Its coverage is a bit hit and miss at present, but the site is free to access and provides images of the stones that have been recorded.

FindmyPast Ireland has some offerings, via its 'Memorials of the Dead: Galway & Mayo', 'Tipperary Clans Archive' and 'Cantwell's Memorials of the Dead' collections. Finally, the Ireland Gravestones Index at **www.irish-world.com/gravestones/index.cfm** is expensive, but has some 407,000 all-Ireland inscriptions.

Wills and probate

Prior to 1858 the probate process – the legal act of administering a deceased person's remaining estate and conveying it to the next of kin (or otherwise) – was one that was carried out by the ecclesiastical courts of the Church of Ireland. If a person died and left a will expressing a wish for his or her estate to be passed on to named beneficiaries, he or she was said to have died 'testate', and the court documents confirming the process were called 'grants of probate'. If a person did not leave a will, however, an inventory of the deceased's possessions could instead be recorded and also brought before a court, which would determine where the estate should go. In this case the deceased was said to be 'intestate' and the legal documentation would be in the form of 'letters of administration'.

The highest of the church courts was the Prerogative Court of the Archbishop of Armagh, but claims could also be dealt with on a more local level through 'consistorial courts' based within each Anglican diocese across the country. Unfortunately, the Four Courts Fire of 1922 did a fine job in decimating what was once a rich resource for family historians, and for the pre-1858 period very little original material has survived. Various indexes do exist, however, and most of these can be easily found on websites such as FindmyPast Ireland, Ancestry, FamilyRelatives and Irish Origins. Although the substance of the wills has been lost, the names of those who left estate and its value can still often be found, and in some cases copies and extracts have also survived.

From 1858 the situation improves somewhat. From this year the probate process became the responsibility of the state, through a new civil-based Principal Registry in Dublin and through eleven District Registries. Although most original wills prior to 1904 have not survived, copies of many do still exist as sourced from these local offices. For those that have not, all is not lost, as from 1858 a series of annually compiled summary books also exist, detailing much of the information that was lost. Known as the *Calendars of Grants of Probate of Wills and Letters of Administration made in the Principal Registry and its District Registries,* they name the deceased and the executors (including any relationship between them), dates of death, dates for the grant of probate or administration, and the value of the estate.

These post-1858 probate records are increasingly finding their way online. In the Republic, the National Archives of Ireland hosts digitised copies of the calendars from 1923 to 1982, with the earlier volumes soon to be added to the archive's new Genealogy Portal at **www.genealogy.nationalarchives.ie**. The records can be searched through the main catalogue at **www.nationalarchives.ie/search-the-archives/**. A typical example is an entry for my three-times-great-uncle, Alexander Halliday:

HALLIDAY ALEXANDER W. (981) 22 July
Probate of the Will of
ALEXANDER W. HALLIDAY late of
3 Sinnott Row North Circular
Road Dublin retired Tramway
Official who died 1 JUNE 1947
granted at DUBLIN to Margaret
Martin spinster
Effects £105 18s 3d

It is short and sweet, but with this I can now order up a copy of the original will using an application form found on the archive's website at **www.nationalarchives.ie/genealogy1/genealogy-records/wills-testamentary-records/**. There are two options here, either a plain copy of the will or a certified copy, though the former would suffice for genealogical research.

Records for Northern Ireland are held instead at PRONI, but here too a great effort has been made to place material online. PRONI's website in fact offers two separate databases with probate material. Pre-1858 indexes for wills are included among a range of records in a database entitled 'Name Search' at **www.proni.gov.uk/index/search_the_archives/proninames.htm**, and detailed information on the probate holdings included are listed in a dedicated page at **www.proni.gov.uk/index/search_the_archives/proninames/about_pre1858_wills.htm**.

For the post-1857 period PRONI offers a database entitled 'Will Calendars'. Rather than digitise the original books PRONI has instead created a fully searchable database based on the annual calendars for the District Registries of Armagh, Belfast and Londonderry, though it is worth mentioning that some areas over the border are included within the catchment areas prior to 1922. At the time of writing there are entries from 1858 to 1943, with more to be added, including some entries from 1920 to 1921, and additional records post-1943. One significant advantage of the PRONI database is that for any of the wills that have survived, the archive has digitised them and made them available for free alongside the calendar entry. The database is searchable by surname, forename, registry, date of death, date of grant and through a keyword search, where you can, for example, type in the name of a relative or an area of residence. It also allows you to submit any corrections if you find that part of the abstract is incorrectly presented.

Again, it is worth bearing in mind the United Kingdom context, as many Irish people had estate proved through the courts in Britain. The English and Welsh system of probate is very similar to that in Ireland, being run by the Anglican church prior to 1858, and the state after. The highest ecclesiastical court was the Prerogative Court of Canterbury, and its records have been digitised and made available to view on a pay-per-view basis via the National Archives website at **www.national archives.gov.uk**, though much better scanned versions can be found on The Genealogist (p. 19), which can be accessed also by a subscription. Note that soldiers of the British Army often had their wills proved through the PCC court, so you may well find Irishmen listed here for that reason also. The other prerogative court, covering the north of England, was that for the Archbishopric of York. Partial indexes for its records, which are held at the Borthwick Institute in York, can be found on the National Wills Index as part of the Origins Network (see **www.origins. net/nwiwelcome.aspx**). Additional indexes from some lower church courts can also be found here, as well as on other sites such as FindmyPast UK, The Genealogist, FamilyRelatives and Ancestry.

Calendars for wills and administrations proved from 1858 to 1966 can be accessed on Ancestry via its 'England & Wales, National Probate Calendar (Index of Wills and Administrations) 1858–1966' collection. If I do a search on this and simply key in the name 'Belfast' in the keyword box, I am told that there are over 33,000 records of relevance, while for 'Dublin' there are over 35,000. Simply typing in 'Ireland' as a term reveals over 121,000 entries – so there are clearly a lot of Irish people included!

North of the border the set-up was very different, as the probate process, known as 'confirmation' in Scotland, has been handled by civil courts since the mid-sixteenth century. There are no 'grants of probate' or 'letters of administration' in Scotland; instead the documents are known in Scots Law as a 'testament testamentar' (if testate) and a 'testament dative' (if intestate), and there are some major differences concerning land-based inheritance prior to 1868 in Scotland, basically meaning that you won't find much mention of land prior to this year in the documents (there was a separate process for this). The good news, though, is that there is only one online resource carrying digitised images of these documents on a pay-per-view basis, and that is the ScotlandsPeople website at **www.scotlandspeople.gov.uk**. At the time of writing coverage extends from 1513 to 1901, with imminent plans to extend this to 1925. Again, using the 'Description' search box here, a search on 'Belfast' returns 345 entries, 'Dublin' some 892 and 'Ireland' another 801, so it is certainly worth a look. The majority of Irish returns included are from after 1801.

Biographical resources

The Dictionary of Irish Biography, a collaborative project between Cambridge University Press and the Royal Irish Academy, is an online database available at **http://dib.cambridge.org**, but only to subscribing organisations. The free to access Dictionary of Ulster Biography, however, is available at **www.ulsterbiography.co.uk**. Commemorative blue plaques in Ulster, dedicated to many of the great and the good, can also be consulted at **www.ulsterhistory.co.uk**.

Some individuals may also be picked up by the UK equivalents, such as the Oxford Dictionary of National Biography at **www.oxforddnb.com**, and Who's Who at **www.ukwhoswho.com**, though again through subscribing institutions. An 1878 book by Alfred Webb, entitled *A Compendium of Irish Biography*, is also available at **www.library ireland.com/Biography.php**.

For information on Irish estate owners and the older aristocratic families, Burke's Peerage and Baronetage and *Burke's Landed Gentry Irish Families* can be found at the subscription-based **www.burkespeerage.com**, alongside many free to access articles on Irish peers, Irish chiefs and more at **www.burkespeerage.com/articles/ire-index.aspx**. The first edition of *Burke's Landed Gentry of Ireland* from 1899 is also included on FindmyPast Ireland, as is *Thom's Irish Who's Who* from 1923, while details of many of the Irish gentry can also be freely found on The Peerage website at **http://thepeerage.com**.

Many people create 'one-name' studies to try to understand the origins and spread of particular surnames. An organisation to which many belong is the Guild of One Name Studies, which can be worth contacting if you are researching a surname that one of its members is already tackling. Its website is at **www.one-name.org**.

Arms

If your ancestor was armigerous, i.e. entitled to use a coat of arms, you can consult the National Library of Ireland's heraldry site at **www.nli.ie/en/heraldry-introduction.aspx**, which includes the *Registers of Grants of Arms* from 1936 and 1980 and a guide to what it is all about. Information on the various Ulster King of Arms from 1552 to 1943, as well as the Genealogical Office at Dublin Castle, is also available at **www.burkespeerage.com/articles/ireland/page92.aspx**.

Various plates depicting pre-Partition Irish Arms can be viewed at **www.maproom.org/00/47/index.php**. Glossaries for terms used in heraldry can be found at **www.heraldsnet.org/saitou/parker/Jpglossa. htm** and **www.burkespeerage.com/articles/heindex.aspx**.

Newspapers

The general public increasingly began to use newspapers in the nineteenth century to announce various life events occurring from the womb to the tomb. Not only did they record details of such events when they happened, but they sometimes placed thank you notices for help many days after, and even anniversary notices in subsequent years, providing several possibilities to try to find a record for a single event if it is not forthcoming from other sources. Elsewhere, newspapers can provide information on relatives who emigrated or on those about to depart Ireland's shores for a better life. Equally important is the fact that a good local newspaper can provide much-needed context to the daily grind of people's lives, and on occasion relate everyday stories directly involving our relatives, sometimes even naming them in the process.

From the *Munster Express*, for example, I have located many, many intimations of vital events concerning my wife's family in Counties Tipperary and Kilkenny, including a detailed account of her parents' wedding day in Piltown in 1960. There is also evidence that my wife's grandfather was involved in a workers' takeover of a creamery in Carrick-on-Suir just prior to the Irish Civil War of 1922, with the red flag raised over the premises and the whole operation to be declared a soviet.

The Irish Newspaper Archives, with newspapers from across Ireland.

In the same paper I have also found, from a compensation claim described in an article in July 1934, that during the same war the Free State Army had slaughtered her great-grandfather's livestock in the midst of the Battle of Carrick-on-Suir, and had torn down net curtains from his nephew's farmhouse, bizarrely to make stockings!

Several websites offer access to newspaper resources, but by far the biggest collection online for Ireland just now is The Irish Newspaper Archives site at **www.irishnewsarchive.com**. This mainly carries titles from the Republic such as the *Irish Independent* (1905–present), the *Connaught Telegraph* (1900–present), the *Kildare Observer* (1880–1935) and the *Leitrim Observer* (1904–2007), but also some northern offerings, such as the *Belfast Newsletter* (1738–1799). It is pricey, at €10 for 24 hours access, €15 for two days access or €25 for a week, but it can certainly be worth the investment. The search mechanism takes a bit of getting used to, but it is one of those sites where the effort can most definitely be worth it.

An index to the earliest editions of the *Belfast Newsletter* is also available online from 1737 to 1800 at **www.ucs.louisiana.edu/bnl/**, though there are gaps in the coverage, particularly from 1737 to 1750. Digitised editions of the *Belfast Newsletter* are also already available on Ancestry from 1738 to 1925, but at the time of writing are accessible by browsing only, i.e. you cannot do a keyword search for a particular name. Ancestry has also added a major new database separate to this collection, entitled 'Ireland, Newspapers, 1763–1890'. Somewhat patchier in coverage than the Irish News Archive, it nevertheless includes such titles as the *Cork Mercantile Chronicle* (1802–1818), the *Dublin Builder* (1859–1866), *Meath People* (1857–1863) and many others.

The British Library in London has two online projects, which to date hold just a few newspaper offerings from Ireland. The first portal is the British Library 19th Century Newspaper Collection, which provides access to the *Belfast Newsletter* from 1 January 1828 to 31 December 1900, and to the *Freeman's Journal* from 1 January 1820 to 29 September 1900. Previously accessible to the public as a subscription-based site, access is now only available from some subscribing archives and libraries. The site holds considerably more titles from Britain, which often picked up on stories in Ireland and carried them also.

More recently the British Library has gone into partnership with Brightsolid Ltd to create a new project, The British Newspaper Archive, at **www.britishnewspaperarchive.co.uk**. Its Irish holdings to date are limited compared to those from Britain, but at the time of writing it provided access to the *Belfast Morning News* from 1879, the *Belfast*

Newsletter from 1828 to 1900, the *Cork Examiner* from 1841 to 1926, and the *Freeman's Journal* from 1820 to 1900.

Although Ancestry offers some partial coverage from the *Irish Times*, the newspaper has its own online subscription-based archive at **www.irishtimes.com/search**, which covers the period from 1859 to the present day. Again it is quite pricey, at €10 a day, €26 for a week or €65 for a year, but with sixteen million articles may well be worth it. At the time of writing, however, free access was available via Fingal County Library (see p. 137).

Also available, and completely free of charge, is the *Belfast Gazette*. This title was first published on 7 June 1921, and acts as the official newspaper of state for Northern Ireland. Prior to this the state paper for the whole of Ireland was the *Dublin Gazette*, first established in 1706; with the advent of Partition this was replaced by *Iris Ofigiúil*, which continued to represent the counties of the modern Republic only. The *Belfast Gazette* is available at **www.belfast-gazette.co.uk** and includes all sorts of material, from announcements of business partnerships and bankruptcies to planning permission applications and military promotions. An archive database for *Iris Oifigiúil* is online, but from 2002 onwards only – it can be found at **www.irisoifigiuil.ie**.

As well as digitised newspaper databases online, you will also find some useful transcription efforts. An interesting site is that of the Glenravel Local History Project in Belfast, for example, which has a 'timeline' available at **www.glenravel.com/belfast-timeline.html**. This is essentially a series of free to access PDF files broken down into decades, which reproduce newspaper stories from the 1830s to 1941. Also for the north, Eddie Connolly should be saluted for his amazing effort, Eddie's Extracts, available at **http://freepages.genealogy.rootsweb.ancestry.com/~econnolly/**. The site contains many newspaper intimations for births, marriages and deaths, as drawn from titles such as the *Belfast Telegraph*, *The Witness*, the *Banner of Ulster*, the *Northern Whig*, the *Lisburn Standard*, and many others from the north. The Ireland Old News site is very hit or miss in its coverage for the island, but is worth a look at **www.irelandoldnews.com**.

FindmyPast Ireland's 'Tipperary Clans Archive' page at **www.findmypast.ie/content/tipperary-clans-archives** is an all-Ireland project fulfilling a similar function with deaths/funerals notices, obituaries and burial information. The site also hosts 'Byrne's Irish Times Abstracts 1859–1901', comprising similar intimations for Dublin City and its southern suburbs, though the database also includes names for additional social and property-based categories. Nick Reddan's site at **http://members.iinet.**

net.au/~nickred/newspaper carries similar offerings mainly for Dublin and Limerick. Some items from the *Connaught Journal* of 1823 and 1840 can be found at **http://celticcousins.net/ireland**, while several titles from Waterford are available online for free at **www.waterfordcounty library.ie/en/localstudies/newspapers/dungarvanleaderonline**, including the *Dungarvan Leader*, the *Waterford Mail*, the *Waterford Mirror* and the *Munster Express*.

Books and periodicals
Many other sites have a wealth of digitised books and journals, with the largest collections being held online by Google Books (**http://books. google.co.uk**) and the Internet Archive (**www.archive.org**). Also worth consultation are Project Gutenberg (**www.gutenberg.org**) and Scribd (**www.scribd.com**).

Villanova University's Falvey Memorial Library has the Joseph McGarrity Newspapers Collection, with some interesting holdings at **http://tinyurl.com/mcgarritynewspapers**, but for academic holdings one of the best resources is the JSTOR Early Journals portal at **www.jstor.org/ action/showAdvancedSearch**. This contains articles from some 200 journals published prior to 1923 in the United States and before 1870 elsewhere in the world (for copyright reasons), with all sorts of Irish offerings such as the *Belfast Monthly Magazine* (1808–1814), *Transactions of the Kilkenny Archaeological Society* (1850–1853), the *Dublin Penny Journal* (1832–1836), and the *Journal of the Royal Historical and Archaeological Association of Ireland* (1870–1889). Early articles are free to view in their entirety, but those after 1870 or 1923 (depending on their source) will only offer the first page – nevertheless, in such circumstances this is still a massively useful finding aid.

Chapter 3

WHERE THEY LIVED

The information within the vital records described in the previous chapter can help us to find clues about not only from where our families originated but also to where they may have migrated within the local vicinity or beyond. Once such places can be identified, additional records may then emerge that can help us to flesh out their stories further. Many of these are now finding their way online, helping us to establish as much about their home environments as their names, ages and occupations.

Census records

In 1801, the year that Ireland joined the United Kingdom, the Home Office in London carried out its first census in Britain, enumerating the population in a bid to determine how many mouths it needed to feed, the size of the pool of available men of military strength, and more. Every ten years from that point the exercise has been repeated in Britain. The first 'decennial census', as it is now known, was a statistical affair that did not actually list the names of those who were enumerated, and it was not until 1841 that biographical details of those within the households were first recorded.

In Ireland, however, the first attempt to create a national census occurred between 1813 and 1815, but was so defective that it was never presented to the UK Parliament nor published. An interesting article on the reasons for the census's failure is available on the University of Essex's Online Historical Population Reports website, better known as 'Histpop', at **http://tinyurl.com/1813census**. The decennial census therefore did not in fact commence in the country until 1821, but, unlike in Britain, when it did start it recorded significantly more genealogically useful information from the outset. The first census on 28 May 1821 asked individuals across the country for their ages, occupations and relationships to the heads of their households, and also established details about properties such as the number of storeys within a house and the amount of acreage tied up in a land holding. By 1841 Ireland's census was well and truly trumping the British equivalent, with Irish people answering additional questions never required across the water, such as the date of a married couple's wedding, individuals' literacy ability, details of family members who had died since the previous census in 1831, the names of absent family members, and more. This additional information continued to be gathered well beyond 1841. To gauge exactly how useful each census was, visit the Irish Times guide at **www.irish times.com/ancestor/browse/records/census/index2.htm#Census**.

Following the 1911 census, however, it all gets a bit wobbly when it comes to the frequency of census taking. With the turmoil of the Troubles leading up to 1921, the plans for a census in that year were in fact abandoned, although a detailed military census enumerating members of the Irish Free State's army was carried out the following year in November (see p. 97). It would not be until 1926 that a new enumeration was taken of the public, though by then the island had been partitioned. Despite this, the censuses in both the Irish Free State and Northern Ireland were carried out on the same night, 18 April 1926. In Northern Ireland there followed further censuses in 1937, 1951, 1961, 1966, 1971, and every tenth year after. The planned 1941 census was abandoned due to the Second World War, but a useful census substitute was generated in September 1939 (see p. 71). In the south, following 1926 the census was taken a little more frequently, with further enumerations in 1936, 1946, 1951, 1956, 1961, 1966, 1971, 1979, 1981, 1986, 1991, 1996, 2002, 2006 and 2011.

Now that you're all fired up and ready to search for the most recent documents, there is some bad news. Due to the private nature of the information gathered on individuals, there are closure periods in operation for most records, which means that at the time of writing the most recent records that can be accessed online are those for 1911. The good news, however, is that the Dáil has signified its intentions to try to publish the 1926 census of the Irish Free State as soon as possible.

Although the data for later records cannot be made public, the reports generated from the later censuses, and indeed all of the censuses taken to date, can be consulted online. Those for the whole of Ireland from 1821 to 1911 are available on Histpop at **http://histpop.org**. Beyond 1911, the same site carries reports for Northern Ireland from 1926 and 1937, and one from the Irish Free State from 1946. Equivalent reports for the south from 1926 to 2011 are available at the Central Statistics Office Ireland at **www.cso.ie/census**. While you will not find your ancestors named in these, they do provide some fascinating context into the make-up of the island across time.

So that's the bad news dealt with. Now we need to consider the absolutely devastating, tragic, rage-inducing, clothes-being-rent-asunder news concerning the earlier records. Prior to 1901, most of the census records for Ireland have not survived. The Four Courts fire of 1922 certainly had a hand in destroying those from 1821 to 1851, but what makes the loss of the earlier Irish censuses even more tragic is that the records from 1861 to 1891 were destroyed many years before through policy. Whether by deliberate order of the government, civil service incompetence or the need for pulped paper in the First World War, the stories about why these returns were destroyed in the way that their British equivalents in London and Edinburgh were not will no doubt be scrutinised for many more years to come. The bottom line is that with just a few exceptions, Irish research is saddled with a seriously major handicap when it comes to the use of historic censuses.

1901 and 1911

It is not an exaggeration to say that the online launches of the surviving 1911 census for the whole of Ireland in 2009, and the 1901 census in 2010,

Online access to the 1901 and 1911 censuses has revolutionised Irish family history in recent times.

have dramatically catalysed the Irish genealogical industry in recent times. The records have been made available online – and for no charge – thanks to a joint project between the National Archives of Ireland and Library and Archives Canada (**www.collectionscanada.gc.ca**). Not only has a genealogical mist been lifted from the country, but various sets of records that many well intentioned folk had previously made available online suddenly found renewed purpose, with the censuses providing an important conduit to help people connect to them.

The original household schedules, completed in most cases by the heads of households across Ireland for both the 1901 and 1911 censuses, have survived and it is these that have been made available for view at **www.census.nationalarchives.ie**. The main home page of the site offers various contextual articles about aspects of Irish life in the census years, but the records themselves are accessible via the link marked 'Search Census' on the top menu bar.

On the search screen there are two options, listed as 'Basic Search' and 'More Search Options'. The first is more than adequate in most cases – if you input too many search terms into the database (and indeed, into any database), you can actually create more chances of your computer missing a potential match. It always pays to try to put as little information in as possible at first and to only add terms to narrow down results if the initial returns are a bit unwieldy.

The basic search fields here are for Census Year, Surname and Forename, County, Townland/Street, DED (District Electoral Division), Age and Sex. If I perform a search to try to find my three-times-great-uncle, Alexander William Halliday, I am in luck as there is only one person of that name in Ireland in 1911. The results are initially presented in an incomplete transcript, which shows him residing at Synnott Row, in the District Electoral Division of Inn's Quay in Dublin, and noting that he is 44 and male.

If I wish, I can find further transcribed details about Alexander at this stage by now ticking a small box above the record stating 'Show all information'. However, if I actually click on his name, a new page is returned listing basic details for everybody within his household. Doing so now reveals his wife Margaret, and my three-times-great-grandmother Teresa Burns (she had remarried by this stage). For each household member the information now presented comprises names, ages, gender, relationship to the head of the household and religion, but I can again tick 'Show all Information' to have the full details revealed. Although this is a bit cumbersome to view, one useful reason for doing so is that you can select all the columns, and then copy the information to paste into a programme such as Microsoft Excel or Word.

However, I would rather actually see the original information for myself, so to do this I now need to scroll down the page a bit further to a panel on the left side of the screen entitled 'View Census Images'. This contains several documents, but the key holding is the very first, noted as Household Return (Form A), which is the schedule filled in by the head of the household. Note that beneath this panel is a link that allows you to view 'Additional Pages'. In most cases this actually contains a scan of the back of the form, where you will find the address of the household. In different searches you may find that instead of Form A there may be a different document, depending on where your ancestor was enumerated – this could be a sheet for shipping returns (Form B3), workhouses (Form E), hospitals (Form F), academic bodies (Form G), barracks (Form H), asylums (Form I), prisons (Form K), the sick at home (Form C) and 'lunatics' or 'idiots' at home (Form D).

For most of us the main document will be Form A, which provides the basic details of household members, such as their relationships to the head, marital status, age, occupations, county of birth and more. The 1911 census is often described as the 'fertility census' because it asked additional questions of the wife: how long had she been married; how many children had she given birth to; and how many of those were still alive? In this example, Alexander's wife noted that she had been married for only two years, but that she had had no children. It is worth noting that a wife will usually have had the information recorded even if her husband was away, and if you find a record for the husband only, you will not normally see these details alongside his census entry unless they have been mistakenly recorded. If a woman was recorded as a widow, the information will usually not have been recorded, and indeed in this example, Alexander's mother was noted as such, with the fertility questions not asked of her. You may occasionally find exceptions to these rules though.

A couple of other details are worth bearing in mind from Form A. The head of the household's signature in the bottom right of the page will only have been his if he or she could actually write; if not, it may have been that of the enumerator, who was usually a constable or sergeant of the Royal Irish Constabulary. Also, note that in the top right of the form there is a small section that asks 'No. on Form B', which is then followed by a number. Make a note of this number as it will help you when consulting certain other documents from the enumeration. The entire form can be downloaded and saved in PDF file format on your computer.

There are many additional and equally important forms that are worth having a look at in the box entitled 'Other original census images available'. Form N is the Enumerator's Extract. This lists how many houses were inhabited, how many people were in each household, and how many people there were of each sex and religion. It also usefully pinpoints the various boundaries within which your ancestor's home existed, with information such as the poor law union, district electoral division, townland, parish and more. In the 1901 version of Form N, take note that the 'Families' column asks how many families were present in each house. This can be very revealing: you may find that on your Form A there is only one family listed, but 'head of household' does not necessarily mean the 'head of the entire house'; there may well be other families present, recorded in a completely separate Form A.

A good example of how this information can be helpful lies with my wife's family in County Kilkenny. Family lore stated that the Prendergast family once owned a farm at Killonerry which at some stage in the past had been split between two brothers, one of them being her great-grandfather Thomas Prendergast. In the 1901 census Thomas was indeed found listed in a Form A as a farmer at Killonerry. He was the head of the household, living with his wife Mary, six children and a servant. Upon first inspection this page seems to provide the entire list of occupants for the house, complete with servants, and so at first I might be tempted to think that if the farm has been split, it had already happened. However, all was not quite what it seemed.

On Form A the number '8' is listed in the top right-hand corner beside the question 'No. on Form B'. When I now consult Form N, one of the first columns on this page is entitled 'No. on Form B', with each of the entries in the column corresponding to a different household schedule. If I therefore go to line 8 on this page, it correlates with Thomas's household. Looking further along this line I reach the column marked 'Families' – but rather than noting that there was a single family present in the property (as described on Thomas's Form A schedule), it actually states that there were two families in the house.

If I now go on to look at the separate form called Form B1, the 'House and Building Return', and again go to the eighth line, I can find even more information about Thomas's property. There are several technical questions about the fabrication of the building (the walls, roof, rooms, etc.), the number of windows located at the front, and the 'class' of the house, which can be a good indicator of the family's social status. Under the 'Families' section of this particular form, which here comprises several columns, it again provides details on the number of families in the property, as well as how many rooms are occupied by each, the total number of people in each family unit and the numbers who may have been sick on census night.

From these forms it was deduced that there were in fact two families in the farm in 1901. Looking along entries for line 8 on Form B1, I found two separate lines of information: Thomas was noted on the second line, but the first contained information for Patrick Prendergast, his older brother. The document told me that Patrick and his family occupied six rooms, while Thomas and his family had possession of the other five. A crucial detail recorded on both lines was the name of the landholder, categorically stated to be Patrick for both households. A subsequent search then for details of Patrick Prendergast's household revealed that there was in fact a completely separate Form A return for him, his family and his own servants – and sure enough in the top right of the form, the 'No. on Form B' was also stated to be '8', as with Thomas's record.

In performing a similar search in the 1911 census ten years later a different picture was revealed. In this there were again two Form A schedules located for both Thomas and Patrick at Killonerry, and their respective households. The 'No. on Form B' question on each, however, listed two separate numbers, implying that they now lived in separate properties. This was confirmed when I consulted each Form B1 for the properties, which showed that the brothers were indeed now in completely different buildings, and with each noted as a landholder in his own right. This therefore not only confirmed the family story that the

Killonerry farmhouse in County Kilkenny.

two boys had divided the farm between them, but that the division had taken place between the years of 1901 and 1911. I was later able to further confirm this to be the case with additional records sourced from the Valuation Office in Dublin (see p. 84).

1821–1891 census remnants

Although not much has survived from the earlier censuses, a great deal more information from these exists than you may at first think.

One of the greatest surviving collections is not that of the 1841 and 1851 censuses themselves, but of information that was extracted from them to support applications for the Old Age Pension when it was introduced to Ireland in 1908. Claimants for a pension had to be 70 years old or more, but unlike in England and Wales, where civil registration commenced in 1837, it was impossible to just simply apply with a birth certificate, with civil birth registration not having commenced in Ireland until 1864. There were different ways that you could obtain proof of age, including the use of parish registers (see p. 39), but the 1841 and 1851 censuses were also used. Information from these was extracted for applicants and included in one of two different forms, a 'Form 37' or a 'Green Form', depending on whether the information was sought by Pensions Officers on behalf of an applicant, or by applicants themselves through searches commissioned at the GRO in Dublin. When the censuses were later destroyed, these applications survived.

Copies of surviving application records are held at PRONI and the NAI. They record not only details of applicants but often of the whole household. A useful article on the history of the application process is available at **www.irish-genealogy-toolkit.com/irish-pension-records. html**. The NAI's new Genealogy site at **www.genealogy.national archives.ie** will soon be adding digitised images of these records and other pre-1901 census fragments. In the meantime there are at least two sites currently offering transcripts of the pension searches for Ireland.

Ireland Genealogy (originally called 'Pensear') is located at **www.ireland-genealogy.com** and allows you to search for records from across Ireland by name and county. With the list of returned names you can then purchase a full copy of a record of interest at a cost of £2. If I do a search for the surname 'Watton', for example, I get eight returns in Ireland. If I select William Watton in Londonderry, and pay the £2 via PayPal, I get a document telling me that William was the son of Daniel and Ellen Watton, and that he lived in the townland of Upper Islandmore in the parish of Ballywillan, barony of Coleraine, County Londonderry. He was aged 70 when he applied, and the application was confirmed with information obtained in the 1851 census. The final part of the document has a section called 'observation', which further notes that his parents were married in 1846, and that he was recorded in the census as 5-year-old William James.

Although Ancestry returns information for the pension applications, it presents the records through two separate databases called 'Ireland: 1841/1851 Census Abstracts (Northern Ireland)', containing information on approximately 23,000 people, and 'Ireland: 1841/1851 Census Abstracts (Republic of Ireland)', with information on a further 5,800. The information was gathered by genealogist Josephine Masterson and originally published in 1999 within two volumes, which Ancestry has since digitised. It is worth noting that in Masterson's introduction she states that not all information was extracted from the pension books, the project being limited by her 'to records with enough information to be of possible help in identifying an ancestral family'. The volume for the Republic also contains a name index to surviving 1841 census returns for the parish of Killeshandra in Cavan. It is also worth knowing that one out of forty application searches from the pension records returned information from the 1841 census, and one out of ten for 1851.

In addition to these sites, Emerald Ancestors (see p. 18) also carries some extracted records for Northern Ireland only. When looking for possible returns from the pension claims, it is essential to consult all of these sites, for their holdings do differ in many regards. Returns for County Tyrone have also been transcribed and presented at **www.cotyroneireland.com/misc/oap-dungannon.html**. For County Clare, a series of transcriptions is also available at **www.clarelibrary.ie/ eolas/coclare/genealogy/census_search_forms/index.htm**.

Two more census compilations from Josephine Masterson are also available on Ancestry. The first concerns surviving entries from 1841 for the parishes of Kilcrumper, Kilworth, Leitrim and Macroney in County Cork. It can be searched or browsed for holdings within individual townlands. The second is a transcription of the surviving material from the 1851 census for County Antrim, comprising records for the parishes of Aghagallon, Aghalee, Ballinderry, Ballymoney, Carnastle, Craigs, Dunaghy, Grange of Killyglen, Killead, Kilwaughter, Larne, Rasharkin and Tickmacrevan. Additional transcriptions from this census can also be accessed at **www.searchforancestors.com/locality/ireland/census1851/** and **http://ulsterancestry.com/ua-free-pages.php**.

There are many genealogical heroes in Ireland and Bill Macafee is certainly one of them. His website at **www.billmacafee.com** offers a transcription of the 1831 census for County Londonderry, which can be downloaded in PDF or Excel formats, as well as providing transcripts and links to many other censuses on the web, together with census substitutes.

Roots Ireland has some surviving census fragments for a handful of counties in the Republic at the time of writing, notably Cavan, Galway West, Kilkenny, Laois, Offaly and Westmeath. FindmyPast Ireland hosts the 1851 Heads of Households list for twenty-one parishes in the central part of Dublin City, as recorded in two volumes for the north and the south of the city by Dr D.A. Chart. The records contain the names of the heads of the households; where they are absent, another member of the household is named. Just over a quarter of all those included were women. Further information on the resource is available on the site at **http://tinyurl.com/1851dublin**.

The Census Finder website at **www.censusfinder.com/ireland** is a great tool for locating additional census fragments that have been transcribed and placed online.

British census records

Many Irish folk migrated regularly to Britain for work purposes, such as service with the armed forces, shipbuilding, seasonal labour and as navvies. Others fled to British cities such as Glasgow, Liverpool and London during the Famine crisis, as refugees fighting for their very lives. Many who made it across the water stayed permanently; others returned home when the situation allowed, or when forcibly ejected by the British poor law authorities (see p. 109).

Whatever the reason for appearing in Britain, one positive outcome is that if they were there during a decennial census year, they will have been enumerated by the British. In my own tree, the only census record I have ever found for my three-times-great-grandfather Thomas Graham is that of his temporary residence in Barrow-in-Furness in the north of England in 1881, where he was listed with his family. On the downside, when it comes to place of birth information, you will often find it simply listed as 'Ireland'. This is about as useful as a hole in the head, though you will sometimes find a more specific place of birth listed in prior or subsequent censuses if they were in the area for long enough, so it pays to check them all.

If some of your family did settle in Britain, either permanently or temporarily, bear in mind that the Irish often settled in groups within communities, such as Bridgeton in Glasgow or the slum district of 'Little Ireland' in the Manchester district of Ancoats, and so you may find friends and neighbours clustered together from the same district of origin.

Often one or two members of the family went ahead, settled down and then acted as a sort of reception centre for other members of the family in subsequent months and years, in a process known as 'chain migration'. If your ancestor's record is not too helpful (e.g. 'place of birth: Ireland'), a neighbour's or relative's record may well be more detailed and offer a potential clue to his or her origins, so do browse through the records for the relevant street or district if you can.

Unlike Ireland, the censuses in Britain from 1841 to 1911 have all largely survived and have been made available online through various websites, some for free, but most for a fee. After 1911 the records are currently closed to public view, following the 100-year rule. Also unlike Ireland, the censuses have remained decennial in Britain. None was carried out in 1941 because of the war, though a unique census substitute exists in the form of the 1939 National Identity Register (see p. 71). You will also often read that the 1931 British census was destroyed during the Second World War, but this in fact refers only to the English and Welsh censuses, with the Scottish 1931 census very much alive and well and awaiting publication in 2031.

Most of the main vendors, such as Ancestry, FindmyPast UK and The Genealogist, provide access to transcripts and images of the English, Welsh, Channel Islands and Isle of Man censuses from 1841 to 1911. Ancestry and FindmyPast also offer transcripts of the 1841–1901 Scottish censuses, but without images. The only online repository offering a full collection of Scottish records from 1841 to 1911, and with the relevant images, is ScotlandsPeople (**www.scotlandspeople.gov.uk**).

Several sites also offer free transcripts. FreeCEN (**www.freecen.org.uk**) is a volunteer project with some of the highest standards for proofing transcripts before they go online. Coupled with the fact that the project started before the major vendors showed an interest, it has slightly had the wind taken out of its sails; however, it has fairly substantial coverage for Scotland in 1841 and 1851, while for England and Wales the effort has been concentrated more on the 1881 and 1891 censuses. The Census Finder site at **www.censusfinder.com** also offers links to various volunteer projects across Britain.

Elsewhere, FamilySearch is also offering limited free access to the British censuses though its Historical Records database. The LDS church fully indexed the 1881 British censuses many years ago, though only those returns for England and Wales are available on the site in their entirety. The Scottish 1881 LDS transcripts are available on ScotlandsPeople at a much reduced rate compared to the purchase of an image from the same census.

If your Irish soldier relative is absent from Britain, he may have been posted somewhere around the world. The 1911 English and Welsh census includes overseas postings for British forces personnel, so should be consulted on Ancestry, FindmyPast UK or The Genealogist. FindmyPast UK also has a useful census substitute for soldiers absent from the 1861 enumeration in Britain, entitled the '1861 Worldwide Army Index'. This database, drawn from the April–June quarterly pay lists, lists the whereabouts of about 98 per cent of those enlisted in the army at that time.

There are also several 'strays' databases available of Irish folk who have been located in the British censuses. The North of Ireland Family History Society has a free listing at **www.nifhs.org/census.htm** with over 15,000 names drawn from various censuses. Elsewhere, Irish Origins offers databases at **www.origins.net/IOWelcome.aspx** of strays from across Ireland in the English and Welsh 1841 and 1871 censuses, though you will need a subscription to access them.

1939 UK National Identity Register

No census was carried out in the United Kingdom in 1941 due to the Second World War. However, just a couple of weeks into the conflict, on 29 September 1939, an emergency census was carried out by the British Government for the purposes of issuing identity cards and a possible list for a personnel draft. The records have survived and are not covered by any formal closure periods (as with the censuses) for they were never officially categorised as a census when the legislation was passed for their creation. The 1939 National Identity Register is therefore now available to consult for the whole of the UK, not just for Britain but also for Northern Ireland, albeit by various different methods.

The Northern Irish returns are at the time of writing the only records for which you do not yet have to pay to see. The records have not been published, and so to access them you need to make a Freedom of Information request to PRONI, which holds them in Belfast. The procedure for this is outlined at **www.proni.gov.uk/index/about_proni/ freedom_of_information.htm**.

A useful example of what to expect from these records comes from an application I made for information on my grandfather at his house in the Greencastle area of Belfast. To facilitate the request I had to supply the address at which he was resident in 1939 and to provide a scanned copy of his death certificate. Information is only provided for those enumerated who are now deceased, and for whom the Data Protection Act therefore no longer applies.

The details contained were limited, but in my case were extremely useful. I received my grandfather's name, his occupation and date of birth. He was listed as a branch manager at this point, confirming why he had moved from Scotland to Belfast just three years before (same firm), but crucially he was also described as having been born in 1905. Although Charles Paton eventually died in Donaghadee in 1989, he had actually been born in Belgium to Scottish parents, but the information I had previously located on his birth from other sources was both vague and conflicting. This date, however, was given by Charles himself – and on the basis of this record I was finally able to locate a baptismal record for him in Belgium.

If your Irish ancestor was in Britain during the enumeration, the formal process for obtaining the information is a little easier, but expensive. The records for England and Wales are held by the National Health Service Information Centre, which implemented a publication scheme for access in 2010. This means that Freedom of Information enquiries can no longer be made, and that you will now need to pay for the returns. The fee at the time of writing is £42 for a request, which can be made via **www.ic.nhs.uk/services/1939-register-service**. You will need to enclose details of an address for which you are interested – not a name – and in

The author's grandfather Charles Paton (right) outside his wireless shop in Belfast in the mid-1950s.

return you will obtain details for everyone listed in the household if they are now deceased. Although details for people still living are not provided, you can determine if others were present by looking at the reference numbers (which later formed the basis of National Health Service identity numbers). They are usually consecutive, so if there is a gap, there is likely somebody else who was recorded at the time who is still alive.

Scotland operates a very different method for access. The records are held by the National Records of Scotland, and you will be charged a fee of £13 at the time of writing for each individual that you are interested in, not the household. You do not need to send an address, however, but the name of the person you are interested in, along with his or her date of death. If the person of interest died in the UK, no further information is required, as the NRS can verify the death itself from its own enquiries, and locate where they were in 1939. If he or she returned to Ireland, however, or died elsewhere, you will need to send a copy of the relevant death record. Information on how to make such an application is available at **www.gro-scotland.gov.uk/national-health-service-central-register/about-the-register/1939-national-id-register.html**.

Other censuses

In addition to the regular general population censuses, other enumerations and listings were also created from time to time.

In 1799 an unofficial census of Carrick-on-Suir in County Tipperary was carried out by three gentlemen, Francis White, William Morton Pitt and Patrick Lunch, in the immediate aftermath of the United Irishmen rebellion. This remarkable project recorded the names of 10,907 people from 1,738 households. A brief snapshot of twenty complete households has been transcribed and made available at **www.igp-web.com/tipperary/1799_carrick.htm,** which provides an idea of how detailed the returns were. A more complete listing, albeit one which only lists the names of the heads of households and their wives, along with the husbands' occupations and both of their respective ages, is located on the Waterford-L Archive at **http://archiver.rootsweb.ancestry.com/th/index/WATERFORD/2008-09**. The transcription is carried in twenty-five separate threads on the site, as uploaded from Saturday 6 September 2008 to Saturday, 28 September 2008. Unlike the previous site, this does not list the names of anyone else in the property, such as children, and so is still incomplete. If you are looking for complete information from the Carrick-on-Suir census, local resident Richard Denny offers look-ups by email via **rdenny@eircom.net** from a database version that he has created of the entire resource. The original is held at the British Library in London.

An earlier census of sorts taken in 1659 is available online at **http://clanmaclochlainn.com/1659cen.htm**, covering all of Ireland with the exception of Cavan, Galway, Mayo, Tyrone and Wicklow, with four baronies also missing from the returns for County Cork and a further nine from Meath. The census was compiled by Sir William Petty, and records those who had been granted title to lands on the island. It was later published in 1939 by Seamus Pender of the Irish Manuscripts Commission, hence it is also sometimes referred to as Pender's Census. Links to various other presentations of this census are listed on the Census Finder website. In the seventeenth century the Census of the Fews from 1602 was drawn up under the authority of Turlagh MacHenry O'Neill, and relates to a barony in County Armagh for which he was chief. A transcript can be found at **www.mcconville.org/main/genealogy/ census1602.html**.

Perhaps the earliest 'census' of all was a document known as the *'Senchus Fer n-Alban'*, which is a tenth-century list and compiled genealogy of the Irish who settled in Dál Riata (Dalriada), the Gaelic kingdom which once straddled the Irish Sea from the east of Antrim to the west of Scotland. The name 'Scotland' derives from the name of these Irish settlers, who were denoted as the 'Scoti' by the Romans. You can read more about the record at **http://en.wikipedia.org/wiki/Senchus_ fer_n-Alban**.

Several religious censuses were created in areas across the country at various stages and may be of assistance. Dublin's National Archives website has a 33-page document in PDF format at **www.national archives.ie/PDF/ReligiousCensus.pdf**, which lists the archival repositories across Ireland holding copies of material from the 1766 Religious Census of Ireland, though this does not provide any links to online holdings. However, PRONI in Belfast includes the information for free in its Name Search database at **www.proni.gov.uk/index/search_ the_archives/proninames.htm**. The census contains entries from most of Ulster's counties, with the exception of Monaghan, and additional material for parishes in the counties of Cork, Dublin, Kildare, Laois (Queen's County), Limerick, Longford, Louth, Meath, Offaly (King's County), Tipperary, Westmeath, Wexford and Wicklow. A different version of the same census is also available on Ancestry.

The PRONI website also includes information from two other religious censuses in the same database. The first is the 1740s Protestant Householders Returns for Counties Antrim, Armagh, Donegal, Down, Londonderry and Tyrone, with the site also offering a useful 15-page document on place name spelling changes since the census was taken.

Secondly, there is also the 1775 Dissenters' Petitions list, which predominantly lists the names of Presbyterians who were discriminated against almost as much as Roman Catholics following the implementation of penal laws by the Irish Parliament in 1691. The petition, protesting against moves to further alienate Presbyterians by the Anglican establishment in 1774, was also signed by members of the established church, and led to the successful repeal of the measures in 1776. The records cover the counties of Northern Ireland, with the exception of Fermanagh, and are particularly useful for Counties Antrim and Down.

FindmyPast Ireland offers another useful religious listing in the form of a census of the Church of Ireland-based Diocese of Elphin in 1749. This covered fifty-one parishes in County Roscommon, eight in Galway and a further thirteen in Sligo, and offers details of the heads of each household, addresses, occupations, the numbers of children, adults and servants, ages and religious denomination. An alternative presentation of this census is freely available at **http://tinyurl.com/elphin1759**.

For various other religious censuses carried out in parts of Clare, Cork, Galway, Kerry and Meath, see Chapters 6, 7 and 8.

Census substitutes
The value of a census is that it provides an instant snapshot of where a person was at any given time, but there are various other records which can provide a similar insight, ranging from street directories and telephone books to political petitions. Where population censuses have not survived, these may help to fill the gap, while others, as with the UK's 1939 National Identity Register, can provide assistance where the censuses are still officially closed.

The most useful of these substitutes for more recent times are street directories. It is worth remembering that the earliest directories listed people from the higher echelons of society only, namely the gentry, professional gentlemen and merchants of an area, and that it was not until the latter part of the nineteenth century that they became much more comprehensive. When consulting these works, do take the time if possible to browse through the volumes of interest, as well as searching for specific surnames, for they often include histories and contemporary descriptions of places, as well as beautifully illustrated advertisements and more. Also bear in mind that your ancestor may well be listed in more than one place within a directory, particularly those for large cities which can be broken down into different sections for streets and occupations, etc.

The PRONI website offers a 'Street Directories' section at **www.proni. gov.uk/index/search_the_archives/street_directories.htm**. This contains thirty directories primarily for both Belfast and the province of Ulster between 1819 and 1900, as well as the 1839 edition of the *New Directory of the City of Londonderry and Coleraine, including Strabane with Lifford, Newtownlimavady, Portstewart and Portrush* and the 1840 *New Commercial Directory of Armagh, Newry, Londonderry, Drogheda, Dundalk, Monaghan, Omagh, Strabane, Dungannon, Lisburn, Lurgan, Portadown and neighbouring towns*. The directories are free to access.

Complementing this collection beautifully is the Lennon Wylie website at **www.lennonwylie.co.uk**, courtesy of Mary Lennon, who has transcribed directories listings for Belfast for 1805–1808, 1819, 1824, 1843, 1852, 1861, 1868, 1877, 1880, 1901, 1907, 1908, 1910, 1918 and 1943. There is also a transcribed directory for Newry from 1898, for Waterford in 1894, and a telephone directory for Belfast, Cork and Dublin from 1913. The 'Assorted Years' section is very specialised, listing pages from directories covering just a handful of streets in Belfast right up to 1970, but also worth a look if you have connections to the city. If you are looking for online access to more twentieth-century directories, the 'Belfast Genealogy' section of the Belfast Forum (**www.belfastforum.co.uk**) has many volunteers happy to do look-ups, all of whom should either be sainted or knighted for their efforts. A transcribed edition of the *Ulster Towns Directory 1910* is also freely available at **www.libraryireland.com/ UlsterDirectory1910/Contents.php**.

An equivalent collection of online directories for Dublin will be found on the Irish Origins website, which at the time of writing has just released the first batch of a planned series of 176 directories and almanacs for the capital spanning from 1636 to 1900. The 'Dublin Directories' section currently comprises editions of *Thom's Irish Almanac and Official Directory* from 1844 to 1870 (to be expanded to 1900), with many eighteenth- and nineteenth-century editions of *The Gentleman and Citizen's Almanack* (Watson's) and *The English Registry and Wilson's Dublin Directory* to be added in due course. The site also offers a handful of provincial and all-Ireland based directories in its 'Directories of Ireland' section.

FindmyPast Ireland also offers online an extensive collection of directories from across the island. They are contained within a section of the site entitled 'Newspapers, Directories and Social History', and as the title suggests there are some records which are not directories at all, such as the 'Deserted Children, Dublin collection', which lists some 500 children taken into the care by the Dublin Metropolitan Police Force between 1850 and 1854. Among the directories are several editions of the

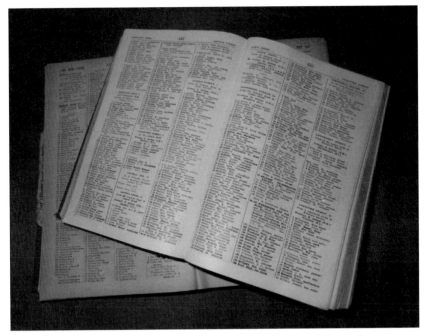

Digitised street directories are increasingly being made available online.

all-Ireland *Slater's National Directory* for 1846, 1870, 1881 and 1894, as well as provincial guides and other sources for cities such as Sligo, Waterford, Limerick, Cork and Dublin.

Additional transcribed directories for Clare, Galway, Limerick, Mayo and Roscommon can be found at **http://celticcousins.net/ireland**, while several directories for the Waterford area from 1824, 1839, 1846, 1856, 1877, 1881, 1894 and 1909–1910 are available in a database that can be searched at **www.waterfordcountylibrary.ie/en/familyhistory/trade directories/**. These also contain some records for Kilkenny, Tipperary, and the south east of Ireland. For Clare, visit **www.clarelibrary.ie/eolas/ coclare/genealogy/genealog.htm** for offerings from 1788 to 1893.

Several other directories can be accessed via the Census Finder website at **www.censusfinder.com/ireland** or via The Irish Archives at **www.theirisharchives.com/categories/view/37/Directories**. An all-Ireland directory from 1862 is at **www.libraryireland.com/Genealogy.php**, while additional resources can be found via sites such as Fáilte Romhat (**www.failteromhat.com**), Irish Family Research (**www.irishfamily research.co.uk**) and Ancestry Ireland (**www.ancestryireland.com/ database.php**). Don't forget to consult Google Books (**http://books. google.ie** or **http://books.google.co.uk**), where you will find free to view copies of directories such as *Thom's Directory of Ireland* from 1850 and *Slater's National Directory* from 1846.

Ancestry has very little street directory material for Ireland (an exception being *Thom's Directory* from 1904), though there are some other interesting inclusions. The site's 'U.K. and U.S. Directories, 1680–1830' collection is mentioned on the list of directories within the platform's Northern Ireland section, though its main Irish contribution actually seems to be a collection of 157 subscription lists for publications printed in Dublin in the eighteenth century. A few listings from some early nineteenth-century commercial directories are also included. The vendor is somewhat geographically challenged with its separate 'U.K., City and County Directories, 1600s–1900s' collection, however, as this appears to only contain records from Britain.

Where Ancestry really does excel, however, is with an extensive collection of phone directories within its 'British Phone Books 1880–1984' collection. This contains a directory for Dublin from 1880, all-Ireland directories from 1896 and regularly from 1900–1911 up to Partition, a directory for Belfast, Dublin and Cork from 1920, and from 1922 onwards a very good run of volumes for Northern Ireland.

Another exciting project from Ancestry, currently under way at the time of writing, is the conservation, digitisation and indexing of 'Lord Viscount Morpeth's Testimonial Roll', a major resource from 1841 which will act as an impressive census substitute when it goes online in 2013. The roll, dedicated as 'The Address of the Nobility, Gentry, Clergy, Merchants, Traders & the People of Ireland', is a 412-metre-long testimonial which records the names of some 250,000 people who signed the document to mark the departure of Yorkshire-born aristocrat George Howard, Lord Morpeth, as the Chief Secretary for Ireland. The document was presented to him at a ceremony in Dublin and then packed into a mahogany box and sent to his family home, Castle Howard in North Yorkshire. It remained in the castle's archive until 2009, at which point it was sent for conservation to the National University of Ireland at Maynooth, with whom Ancestry has been collaborating on the project.

Following on from street directories, another regular collection created annually is that of freeholders' records and poll books showing who was entitled to vote, as well as later electoral registers.

For the north, PRONI has made available a series of free to access and fully searchable Freeholders' Registers and Poll Books from 1710 to 1840 at **www.proni.gov.uk/index/search_the_archives/freeholders_records. htm**.

The records show those who were entitled to vote, based on a property qualification, and in some cases how they voted. From 1727 only Protestants could vote if they held land with an annual rating of 40 shillings, but this was extended in 1793 to include Roman Catholics. In 1829, however, the rate was drastically upped to an annual value of £10, effectively disenfranchising the 40 shilling landholders, and shifting the vote entirely towards the landed classes. The secret ballot, introduced in 1872, ended the need to record how a candidate voted, and from this point onwards electoral registers were introduced. Counties Armagh and Down are by far the best represented areas in the database, with many separate lists, while there are only three lists from Fermanagh (1747–1763, 1788 and 1796–1802), one from Cavan (1761), one from Donegal (1761–1775), four from Londonderry (three for the city from 1832 and one for the county from 1832), one from Tyrone (1795–1798) and one for Antrim (1776). Belfast has two separate lists of voters from 1837. The records can be searched by names and addresses, or can be browsed.

For more recent times, the British Library in London is currently working with FindmyPast UK to digitise its electoral rolls from 1832 onwards, to cover about a century's worth of material. How much of this will include Ireland is as yet unknown, but the records are expected to be made available online in 2013. Various partial transcriptions of voter rolls are listed in Chapters 5–8. If records for an area cannot be found online, the ProGenealogists database at **www.progenealogists.com/ireland/ freeholdersdata.asp** notes the locations of various printed collections known to exist for Irish freeholders, freemen and voters from 1234 to 1978, some of which can be ordered from the Family History Library in Utah and sent to your nearest family history centre.

An interesting online collection is a database on FindmyPast Ireland drawn from the *Reports from Committees, Fictitious Votes (Ireland), Select Committee on Fictitious Votes, 1837–1838*. This was created following the 1832 electoral reform act which dramatically extended the franchise across Ireland. Concerned with fraudulent voter registration, the authorities created registers under the authority of the parliamentary 'Fictitious Votes Committee', with this particular collection containing names from some 52,600 people so registered between 1832 and 1837 (most notably for the Dublin area). A breakdown of all areas included is found at **http://tinyurl.com/ficitiousvotersregisters**.

Three useful online examples of political petitions gathered for very different reasons are the Ulster Covenant of 1912, the Cormack Petition of 1858 and the William Smith O'Brien Petition of 1848. The Ulster Covenant was a document signed by Irish Protestants concerned at the forthcoming prospects of devolution to Ireland in 1912. The rationale of the Unionist psyche was that 'Home Rule' would equate to 'Rome Rule', where the Protestant community would become a religious minority. While the covenant itself was signed by the menfolk, a similar document called the Declaration of Loyalty was signed by women on the same day, 28 September, expressing the same concerns. The background to the politics of the time can be examined on the PRONI site at **www.proni. gov.uk/index/search_the_archives/ulster_covenant.htm**, but the archive has also rather brilliantly digitised the original documents and made them available on its site for free. Note that the signing did not just take place in Ireland, but around the world – for example, nine gentlemen signed the protest in China's Kiangsu Province, in the town of Nanking. Before anyone gets too excited, they weren't members of China's first Orange lodge, but mainly sailors serving on board HMS *Monmouth*! However, for those who signed it outside Ireland, the address area that they were asked to fill in was sometimes instead completed with the name of the parish in Ireland whence they came. When my great-grandfather, Robert Currie, signed it in Glasgow, for example, he noted his address as Knockloughrim, in County Londonderry (the 1911 census in the previous year had simply noted 'Ireland' as his birthplace). The presence of the original signatures can also be extremely useful. That of my great-great-grandfather Edwin Graham, for example, later became crucial in allowing me to confirm that he was the father of a John Graham found in a military service record on Ancestry (see p. 95). One of the documents included in the record was a letter from Edwin to John's superior officer over a medal that was to be despatched – the final line, 'Yours sincerely Edwin Graham', provided a perfect match for the signature found on both the Covenant and the 1911 census.

The Cormack Petition was signed to appeal the conviction of Tipperary men Daniel and William Cormack, who in February 1858 were found guilty of the murder of a land agent called John Ellis. As well as a review of the case, the petitioners were hoping for a general review of the administration of criminal justice in Ireland. The names of those who signed can be found on four pages accessible from the Ireland GenWeb project's Tipperary records page at **www.irelandgenweb.com/irltip/ records.htm#cormack**.

The William Smith O'Brien Petition, located on FindmyPast Ireland, is a similar beast, having been created in 1848 to try to save the life of an MP who in 1846 had joined the Young Irelanders movement – a group determined to fight for Irish independence. On 29 July 1848 he led a failed insurrection in Tipperary, which later came to be known as 'The

Battle of Widow McCormack's Cabbage Patch'. Upon his capture O'Brien was tried and sentenced to death for treason. A coordinated campaign of 166 petitions signed across Ireland sought to have the sentence commuted, with only County Offaly not participating and with half the entries signed in Dublin. In total, the petition recorded some 80,000 names, some of them also of folk who were resident in England, notably Manchester and Liverpool. The campaign was successful, and O'Brien was instead transported to Van Diemen's Land (Tasmania).

There are many other records that can help, such as muster lists, lists of householders, rental records and more. Some can be found via Google, Census Finder and other locations, while others may take a bit more excavation online. A good example lies with offerings found on JSTOR's Early Journal Content site at **www.jstor.org/action/showAdvanced Search** (see p. 59). If I do a search on this for Raphoe in Donegal, for example, I can find an article entitled 'The Scotch Settlers in Raphoe, County Donegal, Ireland: A Contribution to Pennsylvania Genealogy' within a 1912 edition of the *Pennsylvania Magazine of History and Biography*. As well as describing the history of the Scots who settled in the area during the seventeenth-century Plantations, it also contains detailed muster rolls from 1630, and a list of those who paid hearth tax in the parish in 1665.

Land records

In addition to records noting where people lived, and where they voted from, several other important listings were drawn up for the purposes of taxation. Although not censuses as such, they too can act as substitutes in placing the head of a household in a particular location when other records are not forthcoming. Such records often merely state the name of an individual, and there can be no guarantee that someone of the correct name is indeed connected to your family without additional information to corroborate the fact. Nevertheless they can help to build up a picture not only of who was around but also their relationship with their landlords or the state.

The most important and complete collection by far is that known as Griffith's Valuation. In 1831 Boundary Commissioner Richard Griffith commenced a valuation of all the properties in Ireland for the purposes of taxation, starting with the County of Londonderry. By 1844 he had completed the work for some twenty-seven counties, only to be told to drop the £5 property qualification initially required for valuation and to cover all of the properties on the island. He continued to do so with Munster, which had still to be valued, and then retrospectively to the

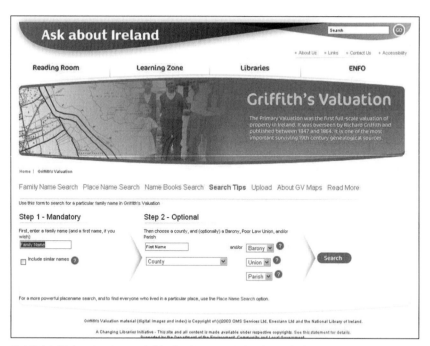

Griffith's Valuation is available for free via Ask About Ireland.

outstanding properties in the counties he had already worked on. The results were published between 1847 and 1864 as *The Primary Valuation of Ireland*. This work is online and in a fully searchable format through various websites, such as Irish Origins, Ancestry, FindmyPast UK and The Genealogist, while various transcribed extracts can be located via Census Finder (**www.censusfinder.com**). The most comprehensive presentation, however, and one which is not only free but also adds a few extra bells and whistles to the experience, is that to be found on the Ask About Ireland website (**www.askaboutireland.ie**).

A click on the relevant link from the home page will soon lead you to a dedicated page that will allow you to search for the records. There are a few searches permissible, as noted on the line of blue links under the title banner. You can search by family name or by place name, with each having a separate search screen, and there are additional options such as a search of the Ordnance Survey name books for an area, and search tips.

If you choose to look for someone by their family name, the database screen allows you to search by surname, forename, county, barony, union or parish – though not by townland, the smallest land division (for details on how to establish the parish from the name of the townland, see p. 90). You can search for an exact name, or include variants by ticking the

'Include similar names' box under the surname field. You cannot search by barony, union or parish unless you have selected a county first. Once you then click on the blue 'Search' button, a page with partial details appears, listing the names of people in the area of interest, the county and the parish, and a series of additional search options for each. It is important to consult all of these. The first option, the 'Details' link, will connect you to a pop-up screen that summarises information found in the full return, such as the townland and street name, the landlord's details, and the publication date. In terms of considering this as a census substitute the publication date is obviously crucial, though bear in mind that publication was not instant and that your ancestor may well have moved on by the time his or her details saw print.

There are then two tools that allow you to see the original information as published, each offering a chance to view the record in a slightly different-sized pop-up window. These windows are a bit fiddly if using them for the first time – you will need to scroll down using the bar to the side of the window to allow you to see the various zoom and pan controls at the bottom of each page, which will allow you to resize the document so that you can read it. At the top of the page you will also see a small icon with a printer on it, which allows you to print off a copy of the document, and two controls with arrows which allow you to see the preceding or following pages. There is no option to allow you to save a copy digitally to your computer, though there are several free to download PDF printer programmes available that can allow you to choose 'print to PDF' as an option.

The published return will offer more information than the summary. The entry for my great-great-grandfather Jackson Curry, for example, shows that he lived beside the National School-House in the townland of Lemnaroy, in the Derry parish of Termoneeny, along with details about the number of acres the property takes up and the annual rateable value. The returns will only show the person who was deemed to be the head of the house or tenant, and no one else in the family, though in some instances you may find the first name of a person's father in brackets after a tenant, if the tenant has the same name as someone else in the vicinity. In the left column of each page is a series of references that can be used to then identify the exact location of the property on a marked-up first edition of the Ordnance Survey map showing the property boundaries (as used for the original exercise). This is where Ask About Ireland's brilliance really shines, for the site allows you to do just that using the 'Map Views' options at the end of each search return. Not only can you view the original digitised map, you can also overlay a modern-day version of the same map over the top and work out how to actually get there. The method for converting the reference of the left-hand column of the printed returns to allow you to do this is a little complicated, but is explained on the site though a page entitled 'Understanding the Valuation and Maps' at **http://tinyurl.com/understandgriffiths**.

The Place Name Search screen can be equally helpful if you don't know the name of the barony or parish within which your ancestor lived, or if you cannot find the individual through the name search. The returns are broken down as far as village or street names, and there are options to further view a list of all names for that area, or to see the relevant map. It should be noted that the main screen offering name searches will not allow for wildcards (e.g. '*les' to look for 'Giles' and its variants). The presentations of the collection on FindmyPast Ireland and The Genealogist will both allow for this, however, if a person eludes you in the Ask About Ireland database. The Genealogist also offers the corresponding OS maps, which can be downloaded in PDF format, albeit in black and white.

The documentation concerning the valuation exercise that is available online is most certainly not complete, with many additional works such as field books, house books and mill books used to compile the original information preserved and available for consultation at the National Archives of Ireland (see **http://tinyurl.com/griffithsvaluation**). Publication was also not the end of the matter, with a series of revision books up to the 1970s recording each occasion on which a property changed hands.

The Irish Valuation Office offers a research service online to help trace property history following Griffith's Valuation, but also from the period immediately before it, from the 1840s to the present day – for more information visit **www.valoff.ie/Research.htm**. Its revisions books are of major importance as they can provide details of changes of ownership and give a description and value of the properties themselves. A change in ownership may signify that somebody has emigrated or passed away, and so the potential value of these books cannot be flagged up enough for genealogical purposes. It is worth noting that if a change in ownership is recorded in a particular year, it does not mean that someone necessarily died in or emigrated at that stage, only that that was when the change was recorded. Using this service I was able to obtain the history of Killonerry farm in County Kilkenny, and as posited from initial research carried out using the 1901 and 1911 censuses (see p. 65), I was able to confirm that the farm was indeed divided between two brothers, Thomas and Patrick Prendergast, between the two enumerations, with the relevant revision book showing it to have happened in 1903.

The records in the north are available up to the 1930s at PRONI, catalogued under VAL/12B, and have been digitised for presentation on its website in the near future. A handy online guide illustrating how to use the revision books in Northern Ireland has been produced by Bill Macafee and can be viewed at **www.billmacafee.com/valuation records/griffrevisions.pdf**. This also shows examples of images from the books, following examples for property searches in County Londonderry.

Prior to Griffith's Valuation the records of tithe payments are the next major resource which can take your research back further. From 1816 to 1869 a tithe payment was required to be paid to the Church of Ireland, which was the established church (and essentially a wing of government), for land across the island. It was fiercely objected to as it was horrendously unfair in its application, with the poor often paying the most. Many people refused to pay, thereby 'defaulting'. The records are not comprehensive – some areas were exempt from payment, including a lot of land owned by the Church of Ireland, as well as all towns, while some parts of the country were not surveyed at all. The records of the tithe payments and lists of defaulters are now widely available online and can also act as census substitutes – although, as with Griffith's Valuation, you will again be noting one person from a household, with no guarantee that that person is in fact related to you.

Tithe Applotment Books from 1823 to 1837 are available at Ancestry (under 'Wills, Probate and Tax' in the Irish section), while lists of Tithe Defaulters from 1831 can be found at both FindmyPast Ireland and Irish Origins, with 29,027 names from Carlow, Cork, Kerry, Kilkenny, Laois, Limerick, Louth, Meath, Offaly, Tipperary, Waterford and Wexford. Based on a list compiled by Stephen McCormac, these are the details of those people recorded by Anglican clergymen who refused to pay their arrears between June and August 1832. A detailed background on the general resistance to the payment of the tithes, along with examples from the original records, is outlined at **www.origins.net/help/aboutio-tithe.aspx**.

Many other lists for local areas can be found online for both those who paid and those who defaulted in their payments. Again, check the Census Finder website and also the various gateway sites outlined on p. 2.

The Registry of Deeds is a major resource based at the Property Registration Authority (PRA) in Dublin, with its website located at **www.landregistry.ie**. First established in 1707 and still in use today, the register holds details of deeds conveying ownership or interests in a property (though not the original deeds themselves), and is indexed by both the names of the grantors of the deeds, and townlands (up to 1946). For research prior to 1833 you need to visit the office in person, but for subsequent years there are various ways that you can request a search, as outlined at **www.landregistry.ie/eng/About_Us/Registry_of_Deeds_ Services/Registry_of_Deeds_Searches.html**. The names index is only computerised from 1970 onwards at the facility, but an online project to index these records is available at **http://freepages.genealogy. rootsweb.ancestry.com/~registryofdeeds/**. At the time of writing over 100,000 names had been indexed from well over 9,000 deeds, not only allowing you to search by grantor but also by grantee.

The PRA also maintains the Land Registry, in operation since 1892, which was designed to provide a more flexible 'title registration' system than the more limited Registry of Deeds could provide. The website provides details on how to access the public register for a fee, as well as a useful interactive map to allow you to search for properties. Based on the modern Ordnance Survey Ireland map (see p. 88) this version is accessible from the home page by clicking on the turquoise 'Search Now' button, and allows you to zoom in and see an overlay of property boundaries for all those registered with titles.

For Northern Ireland, the PRA's equivalent is the Department of Finance and Personnel's Land and Property Services, with a website at **www.dfpni.gov.uk/lps/index.htm**. This provides details on both the

The Property Registration Authority's Land Registry page.

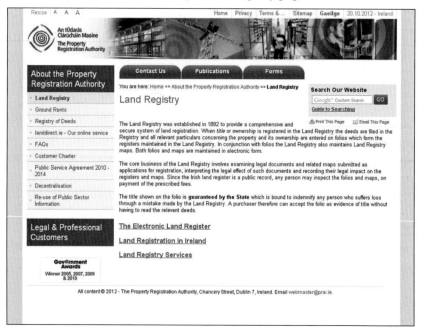

Land Registry and entries from the earlier Registry of Deeds for properties in the north, as well as various research services.

Other land listings

There are several other databases online that can help with research based on land, most notably rental records for estates on which our ancestors may have once lived. The Form B records from the 1901 and 1911 censuses can help to identify who our ancestors' landlords were at those points (see p. 64), but prior to this period Ireland underwent a radical transformation in terms of ownership of land, particularly after the Famine.

When FindmyPast Ireland was established in 2011, its first major database launch was that providing details from a series of rental rolls from over eight thousand of the island's landed estates, following their bankruptcies in the aftermath of the Famine. With the passage of the Encumbered Estates Acts of 1848 and 1849, landowners could discharge their debts by selling their land to the state through the Encumbered Estates Court, and from 1852 through the Landed Estates Court (later sales were handled by the Land Judges Court, from 1877). As a part of this process sale catalogues were produced which included rental rolls of those living on the lands up for sale; these rolls hold the names of more than half a million tenants from 1850 to 1858, as well as details of their rental agreements. In most cases this is all that is left of a former estate's record. The collection contains records from across Ireland, north and south, and can often name more than one person in a family if so recorded on the lease, all of which can be genealogically very useful indeed.

In addition to the above, FindmyPast Ireland also hosts a database of records created in 1907 by the Estates Commissioners' Office, which lists people who had submitted applications as an evicted tenant, or as a representative on behalf of an evicted tenant. The records include name, address, estate from which evicted, townland address of the evictee, annual rent paid prior to eviction, extent of the evictee's former landholding, occupier's name at the time of the application and the reason for the eviction.

If your ancestor lived on a landed estate in Connacht or Munster, or if you are looking for additional information for such estates in those provinces, consult the University of Galway's Landed Estates Database at **www.landedestates.ie**. The site contains basic background information for some 4,500 properties from the 1700s to 1914. Additional rental rolls for northern estates can be found at **www.ancestryireland.com/**

database.php, while a list of rental rolls and other estate records from Counties Antrim, Armagh, Carlow, Cavan, Clare, Donegal, Down, Galway, Kilkenny and Londonderry is available at the From Ireland site at **www.from-ireland.net**, within its 'Genealogy' section.

PRONI's electronic catalogue (see p. 5) also details estate records held in the archive, primarily for the north. In particular its online guide *Introductions to significant privately deposited archives* at **http://tinyurl. com/proniprivatedepositedarchives** provides additional detailed inventories of material deposited in the archive concerning former estates, though it is incomplete. Catalogue numbers for many other privately submitted records can also be accessed at **www.proni.gov.uk/ index_alphabetical_index_to_private_deposits.pdf**. The equivalent page from the National Archives of Ireland is available at **www.national archives.ie/genealogy1/genealogy-records/private-source-records**. A list of various estate papers collections are listed, with further details on some collections available by clicking on the blue hyperlinks, leading to a dedicated PDF file itemising the holdings of that collection.

Finally, a major project currently under way is an effort to conserve a document from 1639 known as *The Great Parchment Book*. Held at London Metropolitan Archives in England, this document was created by the Honourable the Irish Society under the authority of Charles I in the immediate aftermath of the Ulster Plantations, and is effectively a survey of all the estates managed by the London-based society. It was seriously damaged by fire in 1786, and work is now under way to try to restore it in time for the 400th anniversary of the building of Derry's walls in 2013. A blog describing the damage to the document, and the efforts to restore it, is available at **http://greatparchmentbook.wordpress.com**, and it is intended that all information retrieved from the document about local landowners in Coleraine and Londonderry at that time will be presented online.

Maps and gazetteers

Several online mapping sites can help to locate where your ancestors once resided. The Irish Ordnance Survey provides a modern perspective of the country at **www.osi.ie**, this being the same map found on the website of the Property Registration Authority (see p. 85), but without the details of property boundaries. The Northern Irish equivalent is located at **https://maps.osni.gov.uk/mapconsolehistoricalmaps.aspx**. The modern map on the latter looks a little rough and ready, but does allow you to identify individual properties. However, the really fun part is in being able to see several different maps of Ulster at different scales and from various different time periods, namely 1820–1851, 1851–1883, 1883–1920, 1920–1951 and 1951 to latest. Once you have selected which edition to look at, you need to select 'Update Map' to refresh the screen to display it. To use the site you will need to make sure that your computer has Java installed and that it is up-to-date before using. One slightly irritating thing about the site is the slight overkill in plastering the 'OSNI Mapping' watermark repeatedly over each image, to a much greater extent than the Irish OS site from the south does (it carries watermarks also, but they are much less 'in your face') – nevertheless, this is an equally useful resource.

Google Maps is also equally worth visiting, particularly for the more urbanised districts of Ireland, in that once you have zoomed in you can actually see modern close-level photographs of the area of interest taken from above by satellite. The site also offers a 'Street View' perspective, quite literally allowing you a chance to engage with photographic images of properties at street level, and to 'walk' through the street by clicking on the direction arrows highlighted on the ground, though at the time of writing not all of Ireland is covered by the feature. If you really want to have fun, right click with your mouse on the Street View page and you can switch '3D mode on' – but you will need the green and red glasses!

Ordnance Survey Ireland's brilliant map interface.

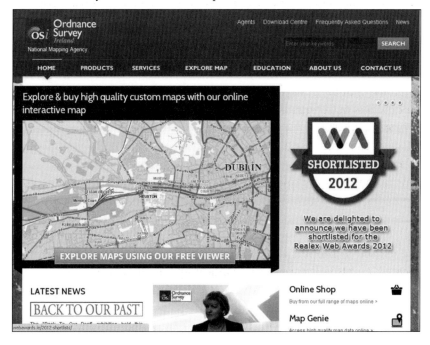

Several free to access historical maps can also be found at **www.failteromhat.com**, including a road map of the island from 1877 and a map of Dublin from 1829, while Geograph Ireland is photographing every square kilometre of the island and making the results available online at **www.geograph.ie**. Dublin City 1847 Ordnance Survey Town Plans can be found on Irish Origins, with a description of them available at **www.origins.net/help/aboutio-dub1851-plans.aspx**.

There are various land-based administrative divisions in Ireland, including townlands, parishes, dioceses, baronies, poor law unions, counties and provinces. The PRONI website gives a good overview of those for Northern Ireland at **www.proni.gov.uk/index/local_history/ geographical_index.htm**, but the divisions were employed equally across Ireland. The 'townland' was the smallest defined area in the Irish landscape, with several located in a parish, often as small as a few acres. In many respects, unlike British research, it is more useful to know the name of the townland than the parish, as it is such an important term within many records. The modern Ordnance Survey maps display the names of townlands, as does the mapping feature on Ask About Ireland's Griffith's Valuation site (see p. 81), which utilises the first Ordnance Survey map. Another website that can help is the Irish Townlands Maps site at **www.pasthomes.com** – this requires an annual subscription, though the maps are also available if you subscribe to the social networking site Ancestral Atlas (see p. 20).

If you are unsure where a townland is actually located in Ireland, there are also a few databases that can help to point you on the right track. By far the most useful is the free to access IreAtlas Townlands Database at **www.seanruad.com**. The site actually displays three search screens, one to locate townlands, another to identify the names of parishes in a county, and the last to identify the baronies in a county, all of them important land divisions. The first of these search tools allows you to type in the name of a townland and establish where it was in Ireland, but it is in fact considerably more flexible than that. For example, you can just select a county and click on 'Submit' to identify the names of all the townlands within, or you can type in the name of a barony, a civil parish or a poor law union, without selecting a county, and identify all the townlands that the relevant division contains.

Ulster Ancestry offers a facility at **www.ulsterancestry.com/ulster_ townlands_by_county.html** which allows you to select the name of a parish to identify the townlands within, though this is for the six counties of Northern Ireland only. Another list of Northern Irish townlands, broken down by county, can be found on the Ulster Historical

Foundation's site at **www.ancestryireland.com/database.php?filename= townlands**, though this will not tell you which parishes they are found within. Slightly more useful on the site is a guide to civil parish maps across the whole of Ulster, including handy maps to pinpoint where they are located. This is available at **www.ancestryireland.com/database.php? filename=civilparishmaps**.

The Irish Times' Irish Ancestors site at **www.irishtimes.com/ ancestor/placenames/** offers a chance to locate place names in the 1851 *General Alphabetical Index to the Townlands and Towns, parishes and Baronies of Ireland*, and the results are presented with maps to help pinpoint their location.

For historic contemporary descriptions of places, Samuel Lewis's two-volume *Topographical Dictionary of Ireland* from 1837 is available for consultation in a website-based gazetteer format at **www.libraryireland. com/topog/**. At the time of writing the second volume can also be found on Google Books at **http://tinyurl.com/samuellewis** and on the Internet Archive at **http://archive.org/stream/topographicaldic02inlewi#page/n5/ mode/2up**.

A *Parliamentary Gazetteer of Ireland* from 1844 to 1846 is also available in three volumes on Google Books. Volume 1, at **http://tinyurl.com /topographyvol1,** covers place names beginning A–C, Volume 2, at **http://tinyurl.com/topographyvol2,** covers D–M, and the third and final volume can be found at **http://tinyurl.com/topographyvol3;** this covers N–Z, and provides an index.

Elsewhere, the Ask About Ireland Reading Room at **www.ask aboutireland.ie/reading-room** contains a whole host of historic treasures for each county in the Republic, searchable by county or subject. These include various statistical surveys of areas across the country in the early part of the nineteenth century (and in some cases earlier). The books must be downloaded, but bear in mind they can be quite hefty in size, in the order of 50MB each. Ancestry also provides an *Ireland Gazetteer and Surname Guide* among its holdings, as well as an 1837-sourced *Ireland Topographical Dictionary*. The free to access JSTOR Early Journal Content carries many periodicals providing contemporary descriptions of places in Ireland (see p. 59).

An 1871 work by P.W. Joyce entitled *The Origin and History of Irish Names of Places* is also available on Ancestry, and can help to explain the derivation of many placenames. If the name of the place of interest is in Irish, you can find an Anglicised equivalent at the Placenames Database of Ireland (**www.logainm.ie**), which also provides an audio recording on the Gaelic pronunciation.

Finally, Wesley Johnston's Geography of Ireland pages at **www.wesleyjohnston.com/users/ireland/geography/index.htm** are well worth browsing through, with all sorts of useful holdings. The site is divided into four key areas, with an introduction followed by sections on physical geography, human geography and political geography. There are maps and statistics here for absolutely everything.

Photographs

There are many collections online that can help us to get a sense of a place connected to our ancestry. The National Library of Ireland provides access to well over 30,000 digitised photographs from across Ireland, in a low resolution format via **www.nli.ie/digital-photographs.aspx**. Additional images held at the facility that are not online but which have been catalogued can also be determined from **www.nli.ie/en/catalogues-and-databases-photographic-databases.aspx**. The NLI also maintains a Flickr-based photostream at **www.flickr.com/photos/nlireland**.

Several commercial sites also offer collections. Ancestry holds 21,000 images from the Lawrence Collection of photographs from 1870 to 1910, just over half of the total collection taken by William Lawrence. The Irish Historical Picture Company has all-Ireland coverage at **www. ihpc.ie/ihpc**, while the *Belfast Telegraph* newspaper offers a service at **http://photosales.belfasttelegraph. co.uk**, with images sourced from many suppliers including the Linen Hall Library. Emerald Isles Gifts at **www.emerald-isle-gifts. com/vintage-irish-town-prints/cavan-vintage-photographs.asp** can also help, while state broadcaster RTÉ also has an archive facility offering stills at **www.rte.ie/archives**.

The author's mother-in-law Pauline Giles (née Prendergast) as a child in Kilkenny, with her grandmother Ellen Murray (née Gorman).

Chapter 4

OCCUPATIONS

Our ancestors will, for the most part, have had some form of occupation to provide an income, whether that be from subsistence farming on soil barely able to generate a crop, to the very running of the country itself. Compared to Britain, however, Ireland had far fewer natural resources that could be exploited during the Industrial Revolution, meaning that much of the benefit of the change affecting Britain in the nineteenth century produced very little yield for Ireland. The country was not completely isolated from the change, however, with some successes, particularly in the textiles industries.

One resource that Ireland did have in plenty was its people, and those who could not find work in their own homeland were often forced to migrate over the water for work. It is fair to say that a significant part of the British communications infrastructure – from canals and roads to the railways – owes a significant debt to the thousands of Irish navvies who helped to create them throughout the nineteenth and twentieth centuries. The British armed forces, which underpinned a worldwide empire, were also heavily populated with Irishmen from the late eighteenth century onwards, whether on sea or on land. The Irish contribution was immense, if not always appreciated.

The following chapter will look at many areas where the Irish certainly did make an impact, and at some of the many professions that were followed in the country.

The military

One of the earliest military records found online is a 1630 muster roll of Ulster, hosted at **www.therjhuntercollection.com**, which contains the names of some 13,147 men. The record was transcribed by Robert Hunter from records held at the British Library, and forms part of an Ulster Plantations website launched in 2012 in his memory, the historian having passed away in 2007. Skipping forward a few decades, if your ancestor was a Jacobite who fought for James II in the Williamite Wars, then consult *King James' Irish Army List* from 1689 on Google Books at **http://tinyurl.com/3zhmnsw**. On the other side, a list of Irish pensioners in William III's Huguenot regiments from 1702 is available at **www.celticcousins.net/ireland/huguenotpensioners.htm**.

Long before Ireland joined the United Kingdom, and throughout its membership (and indeed after), many Irishmen signed up and fought for the British Army. For those who did, various records collections are held at the National Archives in Kew, London, ranging from attestation forms and muster rolls to records of payments and service. The archive has several useful online guides to help you get under way with your research at **http://nationalarchives.gov.uk/records/looking-for-subject/ default.htm** and increasingly many digitised collections are beginning to find their way online. For soldiers serving prior to the First World War (1914–1918), the most useful of these records will be those showing evidence of a soldier being discharged to pension or having served with a militia.

There were two places where a British soldier could be discharged to pension, namely through the royal hospitals at Chelsea, near London, or Kilmainham, Dublin. A small number of soldiers were actually cared for at each institution, but in most cases soldiers would have been out-pensioners, receiving regular payments wherever they elected to settle after service. It did not matter which part of the British Isles that your ancestor hailed from, the place of discharge was basically where you ended your service, with one of the hospitals then tasked with administering the relevant military pension – if you cannot find your ancestor in the records of one hospital, you should therefore check the other. A pension was payable to soldiers who had served for more than twelve years in the army, and as such the records will not contain information on those who left early, who were killed in action or who died early in service.

If your ancestor was discharged to pension through Chelsea between 1760 and 1913 his records should be found in the London-based National Archive's WO97 collection, which has now been digitised and made available online at FindmyPast UK. The records provide brief service details, useful biographical details such as place of attestation and birth, physical descriptions and more. Soldiers discharged to pension at Kilmainham are indexed by name on the archive's 'Discovery' catalogue at **http://discovery.nationalarchives.gov.uk**. The records from 1757 to 1849 have been digitised and will also be made available online in due course by FindmyPast.

The FindmyPast UK collection hosting the Chelsea records is entitled 'British Army Service Records 1760–1915', for the simple reason that it also includes a separate collection of militia records from 1806 to 1915, as held at the National Archives under WO96. Most men were obliged to serve in the militias prior to the twentieth century, and again the Irish were well represented, with some 10 per cent of those who joined the Scottish militia regiments, for example, actually hailing from Ireland originally. As with the Chelsea records, the militia records offer details on military service, but also on employment prior to service with the relevant unit.

Staying with the militias, the Origins Network's Irish Origins website also has a 'Militia Attestations Index' naming 12,500 men who served with the Royal Garrison Artillery from 1872 to 1915. A further 'Militia Attestations Index' is found on its British Origins collection, again sourced from the National Archives' WO96 collection, but covering the period 1860–1915 only for recruitment in England and Scotland.

For the First World War Ancestry hosts about 40 per cent of British military service records in two collections, 'British Army WWI Service Records, 1914–1920' and 'British Army WWI Pension Records, 1914–1920'. The rest of the records were destroyed in a fire in Middlesex during the Second World War. Medal Index Cards have survived for most soldiers, and are also available on the site, as is a database listing those who were entitled to the Silver War Badge from 1914 to 1920. This was awarded to injured service personnel from September 1916, and displayed the words 'For King and Empire' and 'Services Rendered'. The main aim of the badge was to help those forced to return home to avoid being harassed with white feathers as a sign of cowardice for not being at the front. About a million servicemen applied for the badge, and the Irish are again well represented.

Ancestry carries a database of the records of the Committee of the Irish National War Memorial's eight-volume *Ireland's Memorial Record 1914–1918*, which lists about 49,000 men and women who died in the First World War. The collection is also available on FindmyPast Ireland. The Commonwealth War Graves Commission website at **www.cwgc.org** lists the names of all those Irish men and women who gave their lives in both world wars, with details of their burial, where known. Some names which have been overlooked by the CWGC can also be found on the In from the Cold website at **www.infromthecold.org**. An excellent project concerning war memorials across Ireland is located at **www.irish warmemorials.ie**, which records not only those who died in the world wars but also those who fought in other conflicts, from the Civil War to active service with the United Nations up to 1969.

In March 2012 the Europeana project visited Dublin as part of a 'Collection Days' roadshow for a major pan-European project to source materials held in people's homes concerning the First World War, based online at **www.europeana1914–1918.eu**. Members of the public were invited to come along and to have historic items in their possession associated with the conflict scanned for posterity, along with any relevant stories. A dedicated page for the Irish material gathered is online at **www.europeana1914-1918.eu/en/explore/collection_day/DU18**.

A deeply personal memento from the war years is a diary that was written by a wealthy Roman Catholic widow called Mary Martin, the mother of twelve children, who resided in Dublin's Monkstown suburb; it has now been published online at **http://dh.tcd.ie/martindiary**. Kept between 1 January and 24 May 1916, it records ongoing messages to Mary's son Charlie, who had gone missing at Salonika while in service with the Royal Dublin Fusiliers. As a historical document, it covers the period of the Easter Rising and the war itself, but was sadly never read by Charlie, who died of his wounds after capture.

For other services, some digitised records have been made available for purchase by the British-based National Archives in its Online Records section at **http://nationalarchives.gov.uk/records/our-online-records.htm**, including 600,000 service records for Royal Naval ratings who served from 1853 to 1923. A more detailed breakdown of online records for both the Royal Navy and the British Army, including for officers, is available in this book's predecessor and companion volume, *Tracing Your Family History on the Internet*. For those with ancestors who served in the British Army after Partition, you will need to contact the UK's Veterans Agency to obtain service records – details are available at **www.veterans-uk.info/service_records/service_records.html**.

Many who joined the British Army did so after attending a military school, either because their fathers were serving overseas, or because they had become orphaned following their fathers' death in service. There were two such schools in operation, the Duke of York's Royal Military School in Chelsea (previously the Royal Military Asylum) from 1801, and the Royal Hibernian Military School in Dublin (previously the Hibernian Asylum) from 1769 to 1924. Two websites provide a wealth of information on both, located at **www.achart.ca** and **http://rhms-searcher.co.uk** – the latter includes searchable lists of all those who were admitted to both schools, with some incredibly useful information. A good example again lies with my three-times-great-uncle Alexander William Halliday, who was born in Bermuda in 1866 (see p. 37). Following the death of his father on the island, Alexander returned to

Ireland with his Dublin-born mother and was later admitted to the RHMS. The online entry for him notes that he was admitted on 1 January 1878, lists his birth date as 16 August 1866, and then states that his father had served with the 2nd Battalion of the 2nd Regiment of Foot – as ultimately did Alexander, later attesting for service on 13 August 1880. Separate lists for individual regiments are also given, which may help with the search for potential siblings.

One of the greatest resources to have been placed online in the last couple of years has been the Military Archives website at **www.militaryarchives.ie**, created by the Irish Government's Department of Defence. This extraordinary site has many wonderful offerings for the military historian, including its 'Maps, Plans and Drawings Collection of Military Barracks in Ireland' and an online 'Military Archives Image Identification Project', comprising a series of photographs hosted on the Flickr platform. It also hosts an extremely useful guide to the offline holdings of the Dublin-based archive at **www.militaryarchives.ie/ collections/offline-collections**, and several online finding aids, such as its 'Civil War Internment Collection' and 'Civil War Operations and Intelligence Reports Collections', accessible at **www.militaryarchives.ie/ collections/online-collections-finding-aids**. The site also offers a Document of the Month feature. If you want to weep uncontrollably, visit the offering at **http://tinyurl.com/fourcourts** to see the 1922 order to blow up the mines in Dublin's Four Courts, an order that has done so much to sap the soul of the modern-day genealogist. If your ancestor served in the Defence Forces or the National Army, and you want to obtain a service record for them, you should consult the site's Frequently Asked Questions section, which outlines the relevant procedure. If he was in service in 1922, the site has made available records from a census carried out by the army on 12 and 13 November that year, which also included inhabitants based in military hospitals and detention centres. The information recorded included regimental number, rank, forenames and surname, paybook number, date and place of attestation, marital status, religion, next of kin details and remarks.

A major project to catalogue and digitise the Military Service Pensions Archive collection is currently under way, the fruits of which will eventually be released online. It will include details on various military service pensions, wound and disability pensions, and medals awarded to those who saw active service from the Easter Rising of 1916 up to September 1924. Recipients included members of the Irish Volunteers, the Irish Citizen Army, the Irish Republican Army, Cumann na mBan, Fianna Éireann, the Hibernian Army and the National Army / Defence Forces, as well as others who participated during the period. Note that while most of the applicants were from the Republic, there were also many who successfully applied from Northern Ireland.

Various Army Service Pensions Acts were passed to give pensions to those who were wounded or disabled as a result of service up to September 1924, or to dependants of casualties. The key legislation was passed in 1923, 1927 and 1932, with the latter act significantly extending the provision to those who had fought for independence prior to 1921, but who had either ceased serving at that stage or who had subsequently taken the Anti-Treaty side in the Civil War. Separate Military Service Pension Acts were passed in 1924 and 1934 for all those who had seen active service. The first Act provided for those who had fought up to 11 July 1921, but who had also served subsequently with the National Army or Defence Forces up to 1 October 1923. The 1934 Act extended the provision to those who had served prior to the Truce, but who had then stopped participating, or to those who had seen prior service but then continued to fight on the Anti-Treaty side in the Civil War. A subsequent Act in 1949 allowed for reviews of cases previously rejected under the earlier Acts.

In a separate project, Dublin-based Eneclann is digitising various medal rolls from the collection, listing all those who were awarded the 1916 Medal (for participation in the Rising) and the Service 1917–21 Medal. The latter was awarded to some participants who did not qualify for a pension, but who could still show they had been involved, meaning that the numbers included in this database will in fact be larger than those claiming a pension alone. It is hoped that both projects will be made available online in time for the centenary commemoration of the Easter Rising in 2016.

One part of the Military Archives site that is already getting many family historians drooling is the 'Bureau of Military History (1913–1921)' collection, a previous project carried out for the site by Eneclann. Established in 1947, the Bureau was established to try 'to assemble and co-ordinate material to form the basis for the compilation of the history of the movement for Independence from the formation of the Irish Volunteers on 25th November 1913, to the 11th July 1921'. In total it gathered some 1,773 witness statements drawn from various groups, including Irish Volunteers, the IRA, Cumann na mBan, the IRB, Sinn Féin, the Irish Citizen Army and more. The collection has its own dedicated web platform at **www.bureauofmilitaryhistory.ie** providing free access to its holdings, which also include photographic and newspaper cuttings collections. You can search for a name in its 'Index of Witnesses' or search

The Bureau of Military History website.

the 36,000 pages of actual testimony drawn from the given statements, though as those interviewed described the actions of many in their units there are considerably more names found within.

Prior to the collection going online, I had found one brief newspaper mention of IRA membership held by one of my wife's great-uncles – but in searching the bureau's records of the Volunteers who served in the Carrick-on-Suir area, I traced a detailed story about another great-uncle, also in the IRA. This story included information about two separate periods of imprisonment, one prior to Partition by the British, the other after Partition by the new Free State authorities, he having sided with the Irregulars, or Anti-Treaty forces. It should be noted there are fewer resources in the collection for those who were on the Anti-Treaty side, with considerable suspicion still felt by many of its members about the State's motives in 1947 when the project commenced.

The main training college for the Irish military today is at the Curragh in Kildare, though this was in use long before the foundation of the modern state. The first modern structures built on the site were erected in 1855 by the British, who were preparing for the Crimean War, but the Curragh itself has appeared in just about every major conflagration on the island over the last 500 years and more. The Curragh website at

www.curragh.info has many wonderful pages on the history of the area, including a look at the internment of both Allied and Axis service personnel by De Valera and the neutral Irish Free State during the Second World War, old photographs of the camp and many detailed articles on its history over the last few centuries. Transcribed headstone memorials from its military cemetery are also available at **www.curragh. info/cemetery.htm**. These contain many military burials from both the First World War (with links to the CWGC website where known) and the preceding century, along with the names of family members who were also buried in the grounds.

Providing a useful overview of all topics military in Ireland is the Military Heritage of Ireland Trust website at **www.militaryheritage.ie**, which gives guidance on how to find records, the locations and holdings of the various museums and libraries across Ireland, and details of various special projects being undertaken by the body. For the First World War another handy resource is the Royal Dublin Fusiliers Association site 'Remembering the Great War' (**www.greatwar.ie**). This contains a great deal of contextual history on the Irish perspective on the war itself, as well as detailed guides to tracing memorials, and an overview of the regiment's own history.

In Northern Ireland, following the outbreak of the Troubles in 1969, the Ulster Defence Regiment was established in 1970, replacing the Ulster Special Constabulary or 'B-Specials'. It soon became the largest regiment of the British Army and existed until 1992, at which point it merged with the Royal Irish Rangers. Wikipedia has a detailed article on the regiment at **http://en.wikipedia.org/wiki/Ulster_Defence_Regiment**, while 'The Last Coleraine Militia' website at **http://ecohcoy.tripod.com/index.html** details the story of the UDR's E Company 5th (Co. Londonderry) Battalion, from 1970 to 2007, with many essays on aspects of its work.

A Roll of Honour for those in the regiment killed during the Troubles is available at **www.theudr.co.uk**, while the modern British Army website at **www.army.mod.uk/infantry/regiments/5952.aspx** provides a history of both the UDR and the RIR, and a more recent Roll of Honour for those killed since the merger.

Troubled Times

A useful resource for those trying to link ancestors to the 1641 Irish Rebellion is Trinity College Dublin's '1641 Dispositions' project at **http://1641.tcd.ie**. This mainly provides statements gathered in five collections between 1641 and 1654 from Protestant settlers who witnessed the uprising, or who had property damaged, but also includes testimony from some Catholic witnesses. Statements were recorded across the four provinces, providing a unique snapshot into the life of those settlers living in Ireland just a generation after the Plantations in the early seventeenth century. The original records have been digitised and can be viewed on the site, though with the difficult handwriting from the time you may wish to use the equally accessible transcripts! Accompanying the documents is a superb range of articles providing context into the events before, during and after the rebellion.

FindmyPast Ireland hosts the '1798 Claimants and Surrenders' set listing many of those who sought compensation for damage caused in the United Irishmen uprisings of the late 1790s, as well as lists of some of the rebels who surrendered. The National 1798 Centre at Enniscorthy has a Learning page at **www.1798centre.ie/learning** which also details many of the leaders, events, flags, ballads and more from the rising.

FindmyPast also hosts the William Smith O' Brien Petition from 1848 (see p. 80) and the *Sinn Féin 1916 Rebellion Handbook*, a compendium of *Irish Times* articles from the Easter Rising which were later reissued in a publication in 1917. This in itself names 6,731 people, 3,000 of whom were involved in the uprising, as well as 1,306 casualties.

The more recent Troubles in Northern Ireland can be explored through several resources. Some of the best include the Conflict Archive on the Internet (CAIN), as located at **http://cain.ulst.ac.uk**, with various databases, resources and more. PRONI has a tie-in project at **www.proni. gov.uk/index/search_the_archives/proni_records_on_cain-2.htm**, as does the NAI at **http://cain.ulster.ac.uk/nai/index.html**. Wesley Johnston's pages on The Troubles from 1969 to 1998 at **www.wesley johnston.com/users/ireland/past/troubles/index.htm** are also well worth consulting.

Crime and punishment

Law enforcement

If your ancestor was in the police, a great deal can be found online. A useful site offering a general overview of all the various Irish forces is located at **www.royalirishconstabulary.com**, providing histories for the Royal Irish Constabulary, the Dublin Metropolitan Police, An Garda Síochána and the Royal Ulster Constabulary. If your ancestor was ever decorated in either the army or the police, the Medal Society of Ireland website at **www.msoi.eu** is worth consulting.

An excellent Royal Irish Constabulary project at **http://royalirish constabulary.webs.com** includes a more focused look at the organisation's barracks, uniforms, RIC humour and more. A dedicated discussion forum that covers just about everything to do with the force is also hosted at **http://irishconstabulary.com**. Among its treasures are images of many former barracks and extensive lists of births, marriages and deaths relating to officers and their families.

RIC service records are held at the UK National Archives, and are to be digitised in the near future, although an index to some 81 per cent of them is already available online via Ancestry in its 'Ireland, The Royal Irish Constabulary 1816–1921' collection. Additional records can be located in the various county-based divisions of the Irish Genealogy Projects Archives (**www.igp-web.com/IGPArchives/index.htm**), as well as the Ulster Historical Foundation's Ancestry Ireland site at **www.ancestryireland.com/database.php**.

RIC officers acted as enumerators during the censuses, handing out household schedules and collecting them after census night. For the 1901 and 1911 censuses you may therefore come across the names of police ancestors on the Form N or Form B parts of the schedules (see p. 63). Police barracks enumerated in the census were done so on a Form H, rather than a Form A, but an unfortunate problem with some of these returns is that many officers were recorded by their initials only. Another resource that can help you to locate officers in the 1911 census is Keith Winters' site at **http://winters-online.net/RIC-Barracks/**. As well as census transcripts, this identifies many barracks' locations, with some additional resources such as obituaries of officers from newspapers extracts to try to help identify some of those simply initialled.

The website of An Garda Síochána at **www.garda.ie** has various useful history resources in its 'About Us' section. This includes a Roll of Honour for all those who have lost their lives in service since 1922, and information about the holdings of the Garda Museum at Dublin Castle. If you wish to locate service information for ancestors who served with the Gardaí, you will need to contact the museum, but the holdings are quite limited, in the form of service records extracts. Only those who served, or their family members, can gain access. Many of the original service records prior to the 1950s have not survived, but the museum has advised me that those that have cannot be consulted anyway, only the extracts.

The Police Federation for Northern Ireland has provided a website entitled the Royal Ulster Constabulary at **www.royalulsterconstabulary. org,** which explores the creation of the force from the northern section of the RIC after Partition. It too carries a memorial to those who lost their lives in service, while the Police Roll of Honour Trust website at **www.policememorial.org.uk/index.php?page=island-of-ireland-roll-of-honour** carries memorials to members of both the RUC and the PSNI.

The Police Service of Northern Ireland website at **www.psni.police.uk** includes information on its Police Museum within the site's 'About Us' section. Clicking on this not only provides information on the museum itself, but also offers a 'Genealogy' section, with details on searches that it can provide into RIC service records from 1822 to 1922, as well as from various printed RIC lists held at the museum. For service after this within the Royal Ulster Constabulary (RUC), the current PSNI museum has a series of service record cards that continue up to 1977, after which they have been computerised, the same situation for records of the PSNI itself, which replaced the RUC in 2001. There is a 75-year closure period for access to these cards by the general public, although ex-policemen or their family members can view more recent records if the relevant proof of relationship to the officer concerned is supplied. At the time of writing, details about post-1922 records access are not in fact available on the website, but the same search charges will apply (currently £25 per look-up). Contact the museum by email via the details given on the site.

Criminals

If your ancestor was on the other side of the law, FindmyPast Ireland has two major collections online to help.

The *Irish Petty Sessions Order Books 1851–1910* collection contains millions of cases from the second half of the nineteenth century and the early twentieth that were tried at the lowest level courts across the country. Each trial had no jury in attendance, and was presided over by a magistrate or two Justices of the Peace. The records in the collection are for the Republic of Ireland only, having been sourced from the National Archives of Ireland, though the site states that it hopes in due course to be able to digitise the equivalent records for the north, as held by PRONI.

Each record provides the following information – the date of the alleged offence, the name of the presiding magistrate or justices, the names of the complainant and the defendant, the names of witnesses, the cause of the complaint, the judgement and the Statutory Act under which it was made, details of any fines or custodial sentences, the names of any parties receiving compensation, and the name of the defendant sentenced. Coverage varies from county to county depending on what

A petty session order book image from FindmyPast.ie. (Courtesy of Findmy Past.ie/National Archives of Ireland)

has survived, with full details of what is available noted on the site at **http://tinyurl.com/irishpettysessions**.

The 'Irish Prison Registers 1790–1920' collection on FindmyPast Ireland, also sourced from the National Archives of Ireland, contains over 3.5 million entries covering the imprisonment of prisoners within various custodial institutions, including bridewells, county prisons and sanatoria for alcoholics. Most records provide details such as the name of the prisoner, address, place of birth, occupation, religion, education, age, physical description, name and address of next of kin, the crime committed, sentence, dates of committal and release/decease. The most common offence recorded, for some 25 per cent of those prosecuted, was drunkenness, followed by theft at 16 per cent and assault at 12 per cent. The collection is again not comprehensive, with some local registers still held in private hands, and records for Northern Ireland are not included.

If you do not have a FindmyPast account, the collection is also hosted on the FamilySearch website (within the 'United Kingdom and Ireland' category), and can be searched by name. The returned index details are more limited, providing the person's name and role (e.g. prisoner), the year of the event and where it happened, age, birthplace and year of birth, brief details of the offence and the relevant accession number for the record. The site does offer access to the images free of charge, but only at designated LDS family history centres. Using the FamilySearch site can be particularly helpful if you want to try to find names recorded under variants using the website's Soundex facility.

Many Irish folk who migrated to Britain found themselves on the wrong side of the law, particularly because of the harsh anti-Catholic laws and the rise of republicanism as a political movement throughout the nineteenth century. The Old Bailey Online website, which carries the proceedings of the Central Criminal Court in London from 1674 to 1913, has a dedicated page, 'Irish London', at **www.oldbaileyonline.org/static/Irish.jsp**.

Newspaper collections (see p. 56) are also well worth consulting for reportage of crimes, investigations and eventual proceedings if a case went to trial, while the catalogues of both PRONI and the NAI should equally be examined. Many of those convicted were sentenced to transportation. The National Archives of Ireland hosts a searchable online database detailing many of those transported in the eighteenth and nineteenth centuries; it can be accessed via the body's Research Guides and Articles page at **www.nationalarchives.ie/research/research-guides-and-articles/introduction-2/**.

Merchant Navy

If your ancestor served with the Merchant Navy, the National Archives at Kew offers several research guides at **www.nationalarchives.gov.uk**. Tracing such service can be quite tricky, but thankfully many resources have now been either indexed or digitised and made available online.

The FindmyPast UK website has three useful databases: 'Crew Lists 1861–1913', 'Merchant Navy Seamen 1835–1941' and 'White Star Line Officers' Books 1868–1934'. Also now online through Ancestry is the excellent 'Great Britain, Masters and Mates Certificates, 1850–1927' database, which includes details of many Irishmen who worked at sea. The collection contains digitised images of original certificates, lists of ships on which a sailor served, and more.

The Irish Mariners Index at **www.irishmariners.ie** contains information on some 25,000 Irish mariners who worked from 1918 to 1921, as sourced from Southampton Civic Archives in England. The National Maritime Museum (**www.rmg.co.uk/national-maritime-museum**) in Greenwich can also help, with searchable archive and library catalogues at **http://collections.rmg.co.uk**.

If you had family or crew on board the *Titanic*, detailed biographical lists are available at **www.encyclopedia-titanica.org**.

Other professions

The following is a brief summary of some other useful occupational resources online. For further details on some of these areas and others check the county listings in Chapters 5–8.

Agriculture

The National Museum of Ireland's County Life museum in Mayo has a site at **www.museum.ie/en/intro/country-life.aspx** with details on both permanent and temporary exhibitions.

The Ask About Ireland ebook collection at **http://askaboutireland.ie/ reading-room/digital-book-collection** also has various statistical and agricultural surveys for some counties.

Architects

The Dictionary of Irish Architects at **www.dia.ie** details the biographies of architects, builders, and craftsmen who were born in Ireland between 1720 and 1940.

Artists

The 1913 guide *A Dictionary of Irish Artists*, written by Walter Strickland, is online at **www.libraryireland.com/Biography.php**. The National Gallery of Ireland at **www.nationalgallery.ie** allows for a search of paintings by artists' names, and also hosts the National Portrait Collection, which again is fully searchable.

Church

If your ancestor was an Anglican minister, the Representative Church Body Library has digitised the very first 1862 Irish Church Directory and placed it online at **http://tinyurl.com/1862churchdirectory**. Several additional Irish church directories are available on Google Books (**http://books.google.co.uk**).

Free to access lists of Catholic parishes and priests from 1836 are available at **www.from-ireland.net**.

Information on many early Presbyterian ministers from Scotland who made their way to Ireland may be included within the *Fasti Ecclesiae*

Scoticanae collection, first published in 1866. The printed works are accessible on both Ancestry and the Internet Archive, and also in a searchable database entitled 'Ministers of Scotland' on FamilySearch's Community Trees site at **http://histfam.familysearch.org**.

The University of Manchester hosts a site for Methodist records at **www.library.manchester.ac.uk/specialcollections/collections/methodist**, while the Wesley Historical Society has a *Dictionary of Methodism in Britain and Ireland* at **http://dmbi.wesleyhistoricalsociety.org.uk** – check the occupations link at the bottom of the page.

Coastguards

The Coastguards of Yesteryear website (**www.coastguardsofyesteryear. org**) is dedicated to telling the stories of those who worked as coastguards on the Irish coast between the eighteenth and the early twentieth centuries. After registering with the site you can post in the forum and search through an extensive database of records, including UK census returns, Admiralty and naval records, and more. There are also a photo galleries, research guides and dozens of fascinating articles on a range of subjects from *Tales and Awards of Maritime Bravery* to *Shipwrecks around the Coast of Ireland*.

Trace Your Guinness Roots online.

Guinness

The Guinness Heritage website has its very own 'Genealogy' section at **www.guinness-storehouse.com/en/genealogysearch.aspx**, which includes a searchable database for its surviving employee records from 1880s to the present day. The site also has a fantastic 'Archive' section, which includes downloadable guides to various aspects of the company's history from its origins in 1759.

Mills

If your ancestor worked in the linen industry, The Irish Linen: The Fabric of Ireland project at **www.irishlinenmills.com** should be your first stop. The site has details on the Living Linen oral history project established in 1995, with a list of mills for which it has a recording in its archive, as well as many resources to explain the whole process of flax growth and linen manufacturing from the eighteenth to the twentieth century.

A comprehensive history of the industry in Ulster can also be found in *The Irish Linen Trade Hand-Book and Directory* from 1876, a useful resource available through the Internet Archive at **http://archive.org/details/irish linentrade00smitgoog**. On Google Books (**http://books.google.co.uk**) you can also find an earlier directory, *The Power Mills Directory of Great Britain and Ireland*, from 1866.

The Irish Linen Centre and Lisburn Museum site at **www.lisburncity. gov.uk/irish-linen-centre-and-lisburn-museum/library-and-research-enquiries** has details of how to gain access to its Linen Industry Research Association (LIRA) special collection. The names of some 60,000 flax growers in Ireland awarded spinning wheels by the Irish Linen Board in 1796 can also be found at **www.failteromhat.com/flax1796.php**.

Miners

The Miners Heritage Trust website at **www.mhti.com** provides a list of mines in every county, with links to sites that can provide more information on a particular mine. Most of the mines on the site are to be found in Counties Clare, Monaghan, Wicklow and Cork, with pits sunk in the search for coal, lead, copper and manganese, among other resources.

Postal workers

An Post's History and Heritage website at **www.anpost.ie/AnPost/ History+and+Heritage/Home** has details about the service's history in

Ireland and on how to make enquiries into family who may have worked there.

Ancestry hosts the 'British Postal Service Appointment Books, 1737–1969' collection, which contains the British Postal Museum and Archive's collection of Postmaster General minute books listing names, places and dates for postal worker appointments. The whole of Ireland is included prior to Partition, and Northern Ireland after. The British-based museum's site is at **www.postalheritage.org.uk**, and includes a downloadable guide on how to research postal family history.

Photographers

For a database of photographers in Britain and Ireland from 1840 to 1940 visit the pay-per-view site, **www.cartedevisite.co.uk**.

Physicians and nurses

For details on the Heritage Centre offerings from the Royal College of Physicians of Ireland, visit **www.rcpi.ie/HeritageCentre/Pages/Heritage Centre.aspx**. The centre has many extensive genealogical resources on doctors from the seventeenth century onwards, as well as very detailed downloadable archives collections lists and an online catalogue.

Several medical directories are available on Ancestry through its 'UK Medical Registers, 1859–1959' collection, while FamilyRelatives hosts Irish medical directories from 1858, 1872 and 1932.

The Ulster Medical Society Archives (**www.ums.ac.uk**) has transcripts of various histories of medicine in Ulster from 1934 and 1967. For information on researching midwives visit **www.rcm.org.uk**.

Whiskey

For a guide to Ireland's whiskey heritage, including many lost distilleries, visit **www.irelandwhiskeytrail.com/irish_whiskey_heritage.php**. Be advised that the very best Irish whiskey comes from Bushmills in County Antrim – you can find out why, and learn about its history, at **www.bushmills.com**.

The poor

Not everyone was able to work at all times, and for those who were destitute the workhouse often beckoned. Following the implementation of the Poor Law Act in Ireland in 1838, the number of workhouses dramatically escalated, though there had in fact been such establishments in Ireland from as early as 1703. For details of the poor relief system employed in the country, and the workhouses there, see **www.workhouses.org.uk/Ireland**. The National Archives in Dublin also has a guide to using Poor Law records at **www.nationalarchives.ie/ research/research-guides-and-articles/guide-to-the-records-of-the-poor-law/**.

The Famine was Ireland's worst ever crisis. A useful article at **http://freepages.genealogy.rootsweb.ancestry.com/~irelandlist/famine.html** contains various maps showing the relative poverty of many on the island, the location of mass graves and British troop deployments, and more from the period. For more on the history of the Famine visit **www.wesleyjohnston.com/users/ireland/past/famine/index.htm**. Digitised images from the Famine Relief Commission Papers for the period from 1844 to 1847 are on Ancestry, while the same collection is also catalogued by the National Archives of Ireland.

The An Gorta Mór website from Quinnipiac University at **www.thegreathunger.org** contains Workhouse Minutes from Killarney from 1845 to 1848 within its 'The Collection' category, and has a detailed guide to the holdings of Parliamentary Papers from the British House of Commons in relation to the period 1801–1893. The original Parliamentary Papers themselves can be accessed at **http://parlipapers.chadwyck. co.uk/marketing/index.jsp**, with the database offered for free at many participating libraries and universities.

Many Irish people who settled in Britain tried to claim poor relief there as they would have done back home. If it was determined that they had no legal right of 'settlement', they could be deported from the nearest port back to their home parishes of origin in Ireland, even if they had been in Britain for decades. The Parliamentary Papers website contains vast lists naming people so removed, which can be found by using its catalogue, though you may need to use various search terms to locate them, such as 'poor removal' and a date range. The earlier nineteenth-century records tend to be more statistical in nature, providing numbers of those ejected from each parish, with any associated costs. It is not until the middle of the century when more genealogically useful material begins to appear on the site. A good example is a 16-page document from 1849 listing correspondence between the Poor Law Commissioners of Ireland and England concerning the removal of a man called John McCoy from Newcastle-upon-Tyne to Armagh in the previous year. Originally from Keady, McCoy had lived in Northumberland for forty-six years, the last fifteen of which had been in All Saints parish in Newcastle, which should have rendered him 'irremovable'. Despite this, he was deported after having claimed just three days' poor relief at the workhouse, causing something of a row across the Irish Sea.

The first detailed list of paupers on the site is that published in 1863 detailing all the destitute poor removed from England and Scotland and sent back to Ireland from 1 December 1860 to 1 December 1862. Several similar reports then follow, with the latest equivalent list dating from 1878. As well as providing their names, the British parish of residence and the parish in Ireland to which they were removed, the reports also contain additional information such as their ages, the number of members within their family who were deported alongside them, the length of time spent in Britain and the causes for their removal. Some of these lists can also be freely accessed at Raymond's County Down website at **www.raymondscountydownwebsite.com**.

The Moving Here website at **http://movinghere.org.uk/galleries/ histories/irish/settling/removal_1.htm** carries a digitised copy of one of sixty-five volumes from 1801 to 1835 recording the names of poor Irish people who were deported from Liverpool, in this case from the year 1834, as sourced from Lancashire Record Office. The site also gives examples of other useful records associated with such cases.

Chapter 5

ULSTER

When people talk today of the province of Ulster, most will likely be referring to Northern Ireland. However, when Ireland was partitioned, so too was the province of Ulster. The counties of Antrim, Armagh, Down, Fermanagh, Londonderry and Tyrone were reconstituted into the new country of Northern Ireland, while Cavan, Donegal and Monagahan became part of the Irish Free State.

In this chapter I have listed some additional resources that may well help with research in the north of the island. The listings are of course woefully incomplete, but are designed to provide a flavour of some of the key resources available. Further resources are held via the various gateway sites listed in Chapter 1, and throughout the book.

Antrim (and Belfast)

The Glenravel Local History Project (**www.glenravel.com**) has a detailed Belfast timeline from the 1830s to 1941, available across several downloadable PDF files, as well as a history of Milltown Cemetery that can be purchased from the site as an ebook. For a history of Clifton Street Cemetery and a list of burials visit **www.cliftonstreetcemetery.com**, while burials in City Cemetery, Dundonald and Roselawn can be freely searched at **www.belfastcity.gov.uk/burialrecords/search.asp**.

At the Belfast Family and Community History website (**www.belfast familyhistory.com**) you will find many photos of the city in the early twentieth century, rare film footage, an exhibition on Belfast and the 1911 census, and a searchable database of 60,000 people from both the 1901 and 1911 censuses, though this is predominantly for west Belfast. As well as the Lennon Wylie and PRONI street directory listings (see p. 76), several volunteers offer trade directory look-ups from the twentieth century in the Belfast Forum's *Genealogy* section at **www.belfastforum. co.uk**.

Belfast City Hall.

Queens University hosts a Book of Remembrance listing members of the institution and its Officers' Training Corps and Air Squadron who died on active service during the two world wars, at **http://digital collections.qub.ac.uk**. The site also carries a collection of personal material from Sir Robert Hart, former Inspector General of the Imperial Customs, Peking, 1863–1908, and the *Edward Bunting Collection*, which contains material relating to the Belfast Harpers Festival of 1792.

Away from the capital, much of the surviving 1851 census for County Antrim has been placed online at **www.ulsterancestry.com/ua-free-pages.php**. Bill Macafee's site at **www.billmacafee.com** hosts many resources including local 1766 religious census returns, the 1796 Flaxgrowers' List and more. The Bann Valley Genealogy Church Records site includes details of many records for North Antrim at **www.torrens. org.uk/Genealogy/BannValley/church/contents.html**. Forty-one out of forty-two graveyards from the borough of Ballymena have been placed into an online database on the Braid Museum website at **www. thebraid.com/genealogy.aspx**, with the site also hosting interments for Clough from 1875 to 1914.

The Glens of Antrim Historical Society has several articles of local interest at **www.antrimhistory.net**, as well as a video tour of the Glens, transcribed returns from projects on clachans and oral history from the area (including Rathlin Island). The Internet Archive is also worth plundering for the north of Antrim (and elsewhere in the county!), with many wonderful resources such as the 1900 book *Songs from the Glens of Antrim* at **http://archive.org/details/songsglensantri00onegoog** and a 1942 book, *The Irish Language in Rathlin Island, Co. Antrim* at **http://archive.org/details/TheIrishLanguageInRathlinIslandCo.Antrim**, which shows how Rathlin's old dialect of Gaelic shared as much in common with Scottish Gaelic (Gàidhlig) as it did Irish (Gaeilge). For my home town of Carrickfergus, where many United Irishmen were jailed, the Internet Archive offers a 1909 publication, *The History and Antiquities of the County of the Town of Carrickfergus, From the Earliest Records till 1839*, at **www.archive.org/details/historyantiquiti00mcskiala**.

Photo guides for Ballyclare's mills, as well as a local history, can be found at **http://dnausers.d-n-a.net/UlsterHistory**. Ballymoney is covered at **www.ballymoneyancestry.com**, where you will find a map of the area from 1734, a timeline, a discussion of famous emigrants, a townlands list and a database of 55,000 records drawn from various sources. The United Irishmen's Battle of Antrim in 1798 is discussed at **http://tinyurl.com/yglgavo**.

The story of the 1606 pre-Plantation Hamilton and Montgomery-based Scottish settlements of the Lower Clandeboye region of Antrim are explored at **www.hamiltonmontgomery1606.com**.

Armagh

Ireland's ecclesiastical heartland is superbly catered for by Dave Jassie's *County Armagh Research Material Index* at **http://freepages.genealogy.rootsweb.ancestry.com/~jassie/armagh/index-page9.html**, with databases for directories, newspapers and notices, and births and marriages. A topographical description of the county by Samuel Lewis from 1837 is available at **www.igp-web.com/armagh/index.htm**.

Hearth tax returns for the city from 1665 can be found at **www.failteromhat.com/armaghhearth.php**, while the history and heritage of Armagh Observatory can be noted at **http://star.arm.ac.uk/history**. A list of Canadian subscribers for the building of Armagh Cathedral in 1857, as well as a list of High Sheriffs for the county from 1714 to 1857, can be found at **http://homepage.tinet.ie/~jbhall/index.html**.

The 1602 census of Fews barony is recorded at **www.mcconville.org/main/genealogy/census1602.html**. For Armagh tales and detailed pages on the townlands of Creggan visit **www.devlin-family.com**, while Creggan History Society's site at **www.cregganhistory.co.uk** contains old school photos, directory entries and further townlands descriptions. Some nineteenth-century baptism and marriage records for First and Second Markethill Presbyterian Church can be found at **www.markethillpresbyterian.co.uk/genealogy.htm**. Tithe Applotment records for the county, as well as other resources, can be found at **www.connorsgenealogy.net/Armagh**.

Cavan

As well as guides for holdings such as newspaper collections, the Local Studies section of the Cavan County Council website at **www.cavanlibrary.ie** has many free to access digitised resources available. These include volumes of *The Breifny Antiquarian Society Journal (B.A.S)* from 1920 to 1933, various surveys and valuations for the county, and several interesting publications, such as Thomas Hall's 1912 book, *The History of Presbyterianism*, and the 1857 book *The Highlands of Cavan*, by the Revd Randal McCollum. The site's 'Archive' section also provides detailed downloadable catalogue guides to various council-based records, from county council minutes and jury papers to poor law union and school records.

A County Cavan resource site at **http://freepages.genealogy.rootsweb.ancestry.com/~adrian/Cavan.htm** has various Church of Ireland Marriage Bonds Indexes for the dioceses of Kilmore (1697–1844), Meath (1665–1844) and Clogher (1709–1866), parish records from the Anglican churches at Ashfield and Drumgoon, and a 1630 muster roll for the county. Samuel Lewis's Topographical Dictionary entry for Cavan is transcribed at **http://belturbet.iwai.ie/belturbettown2.html**. A map of Catholic parishes in the county is available at **www.iol.ie/~kevins/geneo/cat-map.html**.

An interesting essay on the 1689 Jacobite War in Cavan is online at **www.doyle.com.au/jacobite_war.htm**, while the names of Cavan-born soldiers enumerated in Britain during the 1851 and 1881 censuses can be found at **http://home.wavecable.com/~colin/genuki/CAV/Military/BritCensus.html**. The names of voters from Cootehill are available at **http://home.wavecable.com/~colin/genuki/CAV/Voters/1846Cootehill.html** and **http://home.wavecable.com/~colin/genuki/CAV/Voters/1847Cootehill.html** for 1846 and 1847.

An excellent site on the village of Killeshandra, packed with transcribed resources, can be found at **http://homepages.iol.ie/~galwill/**

histmenu.htm, and Allen Beagan's detailed *Genealogy Notes* on the parishes of the county, compiled from snippets gleaned from a variety of sources, are available at **http://members.tripod.com/~Al_Beagan/ tcavan.htm**.

Donegal

Donegal County Council's Library Service site at **www.donegallibrary.ie** provides an online book catalogue and a list of resources held at Central Library in Letterkenny, in addition to branch details across the county which may hold more localised materials. If you have a library card you can also log in to some online newspaper resources and the Encyclopaedia Britannica. The heritage page of the council's site at **www.donegalcoco.ie** provides a list of Irish place names alongside their Anglicised equivalents. If you are a member of the worldwide Donegal Diaspora, have a look at **www.donegaldiaspora.ie** for information on various museums and other resources of interest.

Lindel Buckley's Donegal Genealogy Resources at **http://freepages. genealogy.rootsweb.ancestry.com/~donegal/** is a magnificent resource with almost 3,000 pages of transcribed records. The Donegal on the Net page at **www.dun-na-ngall.com/church.html** also provides pathways to additional online collections, though there are quite a few broken links. The 'History and Genealogy' section of **www.movilleinishowen.com** has some excellent essays on aspects of Donegal history, from *Ancient Churches of Inishowen* to *Traditional Boats of Ireland*. Some useful genealogical records for the area can also be found at **www. movillerecords.com**, including details from hearth money rolls, various land records, Catholic parish records from 1847 to 1866, and more.

Dozens of resources for Donegal can be found on the free pages at Ulster Ancestry (**www.ulsterancestry.com)**, including a list of inhabitants from Letterkenny in 1910, a Donegal muster roll from 1630, settlers in the county from 1613, a civil survey from 1654, hearth money rolls and much more. If your ancestry is of Scottish descent in Donegal, visit the Monreagh Ulster Scots Centre site at **http://monreaghulster scotscentre.town.ie**. The Clan History page may be a bit sparse and a wee bit Sir Walter Scott-ish in content, but the rest of the site offers some phrases of Ulster Scots linguistic origin still in use in Laggan, details on local lectures and a helpful downloadable guide entitled *Ten Step Guide to Researching your Donegal Ancestry*.

If you want to go for a dander around Donegal, have a read of the wonderfully illustrated 1903 book *Highways and Byways in Donegal and*

Antrim at **http://archive.org/details/highwaysbywaysin00gwynuoft** before you go!

Down

The Cross Border Archives Project at **www.louthnewryarchives.ie** is a great initiative being worked on by both Newry and Mourne Museum and Louth County Archives Service. Some interesting pages deal with land holdings in Newry and Mourne and the Encumbered Estates Court. Of particular interest for County Down is Newry and Mourne Museum's online catalogue for its Reside Collection, which includes details on various landed estates papers collections.

FamilySearch's Community Trees website at **http://histfam.family search.org/learnmore.php** also hosts an extensive project for the Newry area containing extracts from newspapers, diaries, and other resources, as gathered by Francis Crossle and his son Phillip – the collection covers the period from 1600 to 1919.

Ros Davies' County Down site (**http://freepages.genealogy.rootsweb. ancestry.com/~rosdavies**), Raymond's County Down site (**www. raymondscountydownwebsite.com**), and the Irish Genealogy Project (**www.igp-web.com/down/index.htm**) all offer many transcribed and free to access research resources. Peter Meaney's site at **http:// freepages.genealogy.rootsweb.ancestry.com/~meaneypj/** has a section on Down also, containing various gems such as a name index to petty session court reports drawn from the *Belfast Newsletter*. A list of High Sheriffs for the county from 1714 to 1857 is at **http://homepage.tinet.ie/ ~jbhall/index.html**.

Down County Museum's site (**www.downcountymuseum.com**) contains two convicts databases of prisoners transported to Australia, maritime photos and other resources. The Bann Valley Museum site at **www.bvph-museum.com** contains a history of Loughbrickland and Dromore, historic photos, and articles, while Carryduff is dealt with at **http://carryduffhistoricalsociety.org.uk**.

For a 1770 map of Donaghadee and other resources visit **www.donaghadeehistoricalsociety.org.uk**, while Donaghmore is catered for by the Internet Archive at **www.archive.org/details/ancient irishpari00cowarich** with the 1914 publication *An Ancient Irish Parish: Past and Present, Being the Parish of Donaghmore, County Down*. The Newry, Donaghmore, Loughbrickland and Banbridge website at **http:// tinyurl.com/yfuuqe3** carries a list of landowners from 1876 and other resources, though many links are broken. For material concerning the

Lecale peninsula, including a detailed list of shipwrecks off the County Down coast, visit **www.lecalehistory.co.uk/resources.htm**. Again, for the story of the Scottish settlements in County Down during the 1606 pre-Plantation Hamilton and Montgomery scheme, visit **www.hamilton montgomery1606.com**.

The history of Drumaroad and Clanvaraghan is detailed at **www. drumaroadhistory.com**, and Poyntzpass at **www.poyntzpass.co.uk**. The Strabane History Society (**www.strabanehistorysociety.com**) discusses much of the town's past, including articles on the Volunteer Movement (1779–85) and the Strabane Corporation. Lisburn Historical Society's site (**www.lisburn.com/books/historical_society/historicalsociety.html**) carries back issues of its journal from 1978 to 2005/6, which can be read for free.

Fermanagh

The Irish Genealogy Project's Fermanagh pages at **www.igp-web.com/fermanagh** contain many directories, maps, videos, estate records and more, while many additional resources and census substitutes can be accessed at **www.rootsweb.ancestry.com/~fianna/county/fermanagh/fer-1.html**. The Northern Ireland Genweb page for Fermanagh is equally packed at **www.rootsweb.ancestry.com/~nirfer** with lists of settlers from the 1610 plantations, muster rolls, freeholder lists, parish records, maps, tithe applotment records and much more. A list of electors from Fermanagh in 1788 can be found at **http:// tinyurl.com/fermanagh1788**.

For over a thousand images of gravestones from across the county visit **www.tammymitchell.com/cofermanagh**, while Monaghan-based Clogher Historical Society's 'Record Index' has many resources for Fermanagh also at **www.clogherhistory.ie**.

On the Internet Archive at **www.archive.org** you will find several titles on Fermanagh, including *Parliamentary Memoirs of Fermanagh and Tyrone, from 1613 to 1885* (1887) and the two-volume *History of Enniskillen with Reference to some Manors in Co. Fermanagh, and other Local Subjects* (1919).

Londonderry

PRONI hosts the digitised Londonderry Corporation Records, as sourced from both the national repository and Derry City Council Archive. The collection includes Corporation minute books from 1673 to 1901, as well as records of the Freemen of Derry from 1675 to 1945. PRONI also carries the *New Directory of the City of Londonderry and Coleraine, including Strabane with Lifford, Newtownlimavady, Portstewart and Portrush* in its Street Directories section.

Bill McAfee's site at **www.billmacafee.com** offers a range of gems in both Microsoft Excel and PDF formats, including databases on the surviving 1831 census for County Londonderry, the 1740 Protestant Householders' Returns for the county, seventeenth-century subsidy and muster rolls, and an 1832 Townland Survey for Derry City (arranged alphabetically by street). In addition he has also transcribed some of the 1860–1930 Revision Books following Griffith's Valuation for parts of Coleraine, Magherafelt, Limavady and Londonderry, and so much more.

The Irish Genealogy Project pages at **www.igp-web.com/derry/ index.htm** have many resources for Derry including databases such as the Flax Growers List from 1796. The Bann Valley Genealogy Church records site includes details of many records at **www.torrens.org.uk/ Genealogy/BannValley/church/contents.html**.

George McIntyre's history of Drumlamph townland project at **http://georgemcintyre.tripod.com** includes details on the war memorial for Castledawson, and names of many people from Bellaghy Town from the 1860s to the 1930s. A blog-based resource for the history of Killowen is at **www.killowenhistory.com/wordpress**, while a database of nineteenth-century Roman Catholic baptisms and marriages from Lavey is available at **www.lmi.utvinternet.com/lgyards.htm**. The Coleraine Historical Society offers a history and many historic images at **www.colerainehistoricalsociety.co.uk**, as well as details of articles published within its various journals. For burials in Glendermott Old Cemetery (mixed denominations) visit **http://members.webone.com.au/ ~sgrieves/cemeteries_ireland_2.htm**.

Monaghan

Monaghan County Library's pages at **www.monaghan.ie** offer a downloadable 14-page guide entitled *How to Trace Your Ancestors in County Monaghan*, located in the 'History & Genealogy' section. The site also provides a list of historical and genealogical resources available at most Monaghan-based libraries, and those specifically located at Clones Library only. There is an online catalogue accessible via the site.

Clogher History Society offers an index for tithe applotment records for the parish of Kilmore at **www.clogherhistory.ie/tithes-pkilmore**.

A handful of resources are available at **www.connorsgenealogy.com/ Monaghan**, including additional tithe applotment records, as well as civil parish maps for Aghabog and Tullycorbet, and entries from Pender's Census of 1659 for the county.

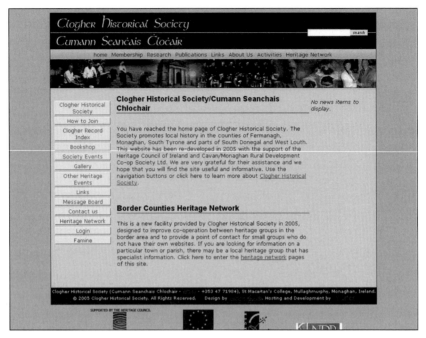

Clogher Historical Society.

For a history of the Deveraux and Shirley families of Carrickmacross, visit **www.shirleyassociation.com/NewShirleySite/NonMembers/Ireland/loughfea.html**. At the other end of the social scale you will find a history of the workhouse at Carrickmacross available at **www.carrickmacrossworkhouse.com**.

Gravestone inscriptions from Donagh Cemetery (1700–1970) and Catholic Qualification Rolls from 1678 (essentially a list of those swearing oaths of loyalty to the county town assizes) can be found on Ulster Ancestry (**www.ulsterancestry.com**).

An 1895 book entitled *Historical Sketches of Monaghan: from the Earliest Records to the Fenian Movement* can be found at **http://archive.org/details/historicalsketch00rushrich**, while the 1801 *Statistical Survey of the County of Monaghan* can be consulted at **http://archive.org/details/statisticalsurv13socigoog**.

Tyrone

The County Tyrone Website at **www.cotyroneireland.com/index.html** has an excellent collection of resources, including various church records, maps, Griffith's Valuation, schools records and more. Ulster Ancestry (**www.ulsterancestry.com**) has various offerings, from an undated rent book for Strabane and land grants in 1610, to several religious census transcripts and substitutes. Although based just over the border in Monaghan, the Clogher Historical Society's *Record Index* at **www.clogherhistory.ie** has many resources for Tyrone also.

The County Tyrone Gravestone Project (**www.tammymitchell.com/ cotyrone**) carries over 1,100 gravestone photos from across the county, while some burials within cemeteries in Cappagh, Dumnakilly and Omagh can also be identified at **www.gravestonephotos.com/public/ area.php?area=Tyrone&country=Ir**. Monumental inscriptions for Leckpatrick Old Presbyterian Cemetery in Strabane can be located at **http://members.webone.com.au/~sgrieves/cemetries__ireland.htm**.

A summary of the *Ecclesiastical Census of Clogherny* (1851–1852) can be read at **www.localpopulationstudies.org.uk/PDF/LPS29/LPS29_1982_ 35-49.pdf**. The history of Bready is discussed at **www.breadyancestry. com**, with the site including a townland map, and sections on Ulster Scots heritage, historical maps, and databases of 30,000 names derived from several sources.

Killeeshil and Clonaneese Historical Society has an archive with rent rolls, census returns and more at **http://killeeshilclonaneese.org/joomla**, while Glenelly Historical Society (**www.glenellyhistorical.org.uk**) has essays on the Great Glenelly Flood of 1680, the Plumbridge Water Scheme and other useful local articles. For the contents of past issues of the Stewartstown & District Local History Society's journal *The Bell* visit **www.stewartstownhistory.co.uk**.

Chapter 6

MUNSTER

The province of Munster, to the south of the island, has its largest settlement around the city of Cork. It contains six counties, Clare, Cork, Kerry, Limerick, Tipperary and Waterford. The following chapter provides some online highlights relating to research within them.

Clare

If you have connections to Clare, visit the County Library site at **www.clarelibrary.ie** and celebrate your good fortune – it may well be the

One of the best local authority platforms online is that of Clare County Library.

Clare County Library — Clare Genealogy & Family History
Home | About This Website | Forums | Foto | Maps | Places | Archaeology | History | Music | Search this Website | Copyright | Visitors' Book | Contact Us | What's New
As Gaeilge / To donate material please contact Maureen Comber

Online Records

- 1901 Census of Population of County Clare
- 1901 Census of Population of County Clare - Surname Index
- 1901 Census of Population of County Clare - List of Surnames
- 1901 Census of Population of county Clare - Frequency of Surnames
- 1841 & 1851 Census Search Forms

- Search the 1911 Census of Population of County Clare (external link)
- Browse the 1911 Census of Population of County Clare (external link)

- 1852/1855 Index to Griffith's Valuation for Clare - Surname Index
- 1852/1855 Index to Griffith's Valuation for Clare - Parish Index
- 1852/1855 Index to Griffith's Valuation for Clare - List of Surnames
- 1852/1855 Index to Griffith's Valuation for Clare - Frequency of Surnames

- 1820s-1840s Index to Tithe Applotment Books - Surname Index
- 1820s-1840s Index to Tithe Applotment Books - Parish Index
- 1820s-1840s Index to Tithe Applotment Books - List of Surnames
- 1820s-1840s Index to Tithe Applotment Books - Frequency of Surnames

- Combined list of surnames which occur in the 1901 Census of Population of County Clare, the Griffith's Valuation 1855 of County Clare, and the Tithe Applotment Books (1820s-1840s) for County Clare, including the number of occurences for each surname collected in each source. (3MB file)
- Names to conjure with: a perspective on Clare surnames by Pat Flynn

- 1692-1775 Freemen of Ennis
- 1768 Freeholders of County Clare
- 1821 List of Freeholders, County Clare
- 1829 Registry of Freeholders for the County of Clare
- 1832 Applicants to the Registry of Freeholders, Borough of Ennis
- 1841 Applicants to the Registry of Freeholders, Co. Clare

- 1888-1916 Journals: Association for the Preservation of the Memorials of the Dead, Ireland
- 1636-1703 Books of Survey and Distribution
- 1659 Census of Clare
- Pre-1855 Estate Papers in NLI and NAI
- 1876 Land owners in Clare
- 1824 Hedge School Teachers in Clare

Directories

- 1893 Guy's Directory, Clare
- 1881, Slater's Directory, Ennis & Clarecastle
- 1880-1 Bassett's Directory, Clare
- 1875-6 Bassett's Directory, Clare
- 1870, Slater's Directory, Ennis & Clarecastle
- 1842,1863 Hogan's Directory, Kilkee
- 1846 Slater's Directory, Clare
- 1814 Leet's Directory, Clare
- 1824 Pigot's Directory, Clare
- 1788 Lucas's Directory, Ennis

Histories of Clare Families

- The Origins of Heraldry
- Principal original families of County Clare
- Learned Families of Thomond
- The territories of the ancient Irish families in Limerick and Clare
- The BUTLERS of County Clare
- Short Study of a Transplanted Family (MACLYSAGHTS)
- The O'DAVORENS of Cahermacnaughten

Donated Material

Transcriptions of material from primary source documents and family histories donated to Clare County Library. See the > Clare Past Forum also for donated material directly uploaded by forum members.

- Births/Baptisms, Marriages, Deaths
- Census Records
- Court Reports (including Evictions)
- Directories
- Emigration Records
- Family Histories, Biographies & Memoirs
- Graveyard Inscriptions
- Military & Police Records
- Memorial / Mortuary Cards
- Registers, Rent-rolls & Leases

best local authority website in Ireland. It is packed with resources, including digitised maps, audio books and ebooks, a catalogue, and a simply brilliant 'Genealogy and Local History' section at **www.clare library.ie/eolas/coclare/genealogy/genealog.htm**, stuffed with resources, such as a religious census of Kilfenora and Kiltoraght parishes drawn up in November 1866, and dozens of other wee gems. Once you go in, remember to come up for air once in a while! The library also has a useful photo collection accessible at **http://foto.clarelibrary.ie/fotoweb/** and a dedicated blog at **http://clarelibrary.blogspot.co.uk**.

A Little Bit of Ireland at **http://celticcousins.net/ireland** has some parish record-derived resources for Clare, and Connors Genealogy at **www.connorsgenealogy.com/clare** has additional materials including some land-based records. Essays on aspects of east Clare history are available at **www.eastclareheritage.com**. Various freeholders and electoral records are freely available at **www.clarelibrary.ie/eolas/ coclare/genealogy/genealog.htm** for the county from 1692 to 1841.

An 1808 work, *Statistical Survey of the County of Clare*, is on the Internet Archive at **http://archive.org/details/statisticalsurv09socigoog**, as is James Frost's *The History and Topography of the County of Clare* from 1893 at **http://archive.org/details/historyandtopog00frosgoog**.

Cork

The Cork Past and Present website at **www.corkpastandpresent.ie** is a gateway site to various resources from Cork City Libraries, which includes both a 'Genealogy' section and a 'Local History' area. In the former you will find various research guides, a list of streets and the district electoral divisions to which they belong, digitised editions of Green's Index to marriage licence bonds for the dioceses of Cloyne and Cork and Ross, and an index to wills for the same dioceses. The 'Local History' section provides information on the Cork Local Studies Department, as well as a useful Cork bibliography and details of local newspaper holdings in the department.

Cork City and County Archives (**www.corkarchives.ie**) has a genealogy section with many digitised resources, including burial registers for Cobh/Queenstown (1879–1907), Dubullogue (1896–1988), Kilcully (1931–1974) and Rathcooney (1896–1941). The site also has detailed catalogue descriptions for the holdings of fifteen poor law union boards, rate collection books, a list of freemen of Cork from 1719 to 1841, and much more.

Resources for West Cork, and Clonakilty in particular, are well represented at **www.failteromhat.com**, including various essays on the areas, maps, photographs and databases of useful genealogical material. Skibbereen Heritage Centre offers resources at **www.skibbheritage.com** including a database of tithe applotment books for fifteen parishes in the Barony of West Carbery, a townlands database, and an estate records database covering eighty-six townlands in the vicinity from 1803 to 1919. It also has a dedicated West Cork Graveyards Survey page at **www.graveyards.skibbheritage.com**.

Rootsweb's Cork pages at **http://freepages.genealogy.rootsweb. ancestry.com/~mturner/cork/ire.cork.htm** are teeming with resources, as is Kae Lewis's Cork Records Database at **www.corkrecords.com**. Ginni Swanton's genealogy pages at **www.ginnisw.com/corkmain.html** include resources such as confirmation records for the parishes of Enniskeane, Desertserges, and Kinneigh, and Cork County listings from an 1875 directory (excluding Cork City). The city entries can be found at **www.digdatgenealogy.com/cork75.htm,** however. Another remarkable resource for Cork City is a list of baptisms from the Unitarian Church from 1717 to 1900, available at **www.unitarianchurchcork.org/Baptism Records.html**. For Bandon resources, including indices to censuses of Ballymodan Protestants from 1834 and 1846, visit **www.bandon-genealogy.com**.

Articles in the Cork Genealogical Society's journals from 2004 to 2012 are indexed at **www.corkgenealogicalsociety.com**, while Mallow Archaeological and Historical Society has a much more packed offering of journal indexes and records at **http://rootsweb.ancestry.com/~irlmahs/**.

The Allihies Copper Mine Museum website (**www.new.acmm.ie**) ventures from genealogy to geology with a history of the industry in the area throughout the nineteenth and twentieth centuries. Finally, if you're researching the 'Big Fella' and the War of Independence, the Michael Collins Centre site has a couple of maps depicting key events in his life at **www.michaelcollinscentre.com/search.html**.

Kerry

Challenging my working theory that God is an Ulsterman, and in fact originates from somewhere in Kerry, is the truly brilliant Kerry Local Authorities Graveyard Records project at **http://kerrylaburials.ie/en/ Index.aspx** (see p. 50). The Local History page of Kerry County Library's site at **www.kerrylibrary.ie** provides lists of newspapers and journals for which it has copies, a database of casualties from the First World War, and detailed descriptions of other holdings at its Local History and Archives Department (the same page is also accessible at **www.kerrycolib.ie/local.asp**).

The workhouse minute books from the Killarney Union for the famine years of 1845–1848 have been digitised by Quinnipiac University and placed online at **www.thegreathunger.org/TheCollection/Killarney Minutes**. You can download the original images or read detailed transcripts of some of the pages on the site. For marriages across Kerry in 1877 consult **http://tinyurl.com/dy7sua8**, and a list of marriages in the barony of Trughanacmy from 1874 to 1884 is at **www.geocities.ws/irishancestralpages/KMmain.html**.

Resources for the Catholic parish of Ballyferriter on the Dingle peninsula are at **http://reocities.com/Athens/Ithaca/7974/Ballyferriter** – this includes useful townlands and Catholic diocese maps for the county, and a list of heads of Roman Catholic households from 1827 to 1852. Cemetery transcriptions from Brosna from 1700 to 1998 can be found at **www.bluegumtrees.com/genealogy/genealogy.html**, along with tithe valuations from the 1820s. A parish history for Brosna can also be found at **www.rootsweb.ancestry.com/~irlker/brosbk.html**.

A register of electors for Killarney from 1926 can be found at **http://tinyurl.com/killarney1926**. The Heritage Centre at Knightstown, Valentia Island, is also worth exploring at **http://vhc.cablehistory.org** for a flavour of its holdings.

Limerick

Limerick City has another great local authority website online at **http://limerick.ie/cityarchives**, providing details on the Local Studies Department, the City Archives and an online catalogue to the Jim Kemmy Municipal Museum. The site is packed with free to access digitised collections, including burial registers for Mount St Lawrence (1855–2008), its new extension (February 1960–April 2010), and for Mount St Oliver (February 1960–April 1998). There are also various local government collections such as rate valuation books from 1893 to 1971, various burgess and electoral lists, and Limerick Police Force records from 1922. The Local Studies section of the website is also jam-packed with offerings, including a list of mayors from 1197 to 2006, various e-books (with some also hosted on Ask About Ireland), various family histories and more. For Limerick City Library's Reference and Local Studies Department's holdings consult **www.limerickcity.ie/Library/LocalStudies** – a catalogue of its holdings is included.

Another great resource for the city is Limerick's Life at **http://limerickslife.com**. This includes various resources ranging from photographs and videos to church guides and monumental inscriptions at Mount St Lawrence. A discussion forum is also present.

Limerick County Council has a separate site at **www.lcc.ie/Library** for its Lissanalta House-based archives and local studies collections. This lists the various cemeteries for which it holds monumental inscriptions, and provides many other county-based resources, including digitised maps of baronies and civil parishes.

Although the Bureau of Military History website (see p. 98) has placed online witness statements concerning the War of Independence, Limerick Archives has also placed online the same statements from Counties Limerick and Tipperary. In using these local collections I have on occasion found some pages to be missing from the statements compared to those on the Military Archives site – however, an interesting feature for this more localised collection is that they can be accessed via an interactive Google Map at **http://tinyurl.com/witnessstatements**, which may provide a useful option if wishing to target holdings for a specific area.

A Little Bit of Ireland at **http://celticcousins.net/ireland** has the names of freemen from Limerick between 1746 and 1836, records for Rathkeale, and other useful lists. For monumental inscriptions in the Anglican cemetery at Rathkeale visit **http://freepages.genealogy.rootsweb. ancestry.com/~joanne/monumental_inscriptions.htm**. Finally, the Irish Palatine Heritage Centre in Rathkeale provides some background to those with an ancestral background from the Rheinland-Pfalz region of Germany at **www.irishpalatines.org**.

Tipperary

The Thurles-based Tipperary Library Service has a platform at **www.tipperarylibraries.ie** where you will find an area called Tipperary Studies. This has details about publications on sale, but also some basic genealogical resources, such as a list of newspapers held in the archive, with relevant date coverage, and a library catalogue. The service also has a YouTube channel at **www.youtube.com/user/Tippstudies** which carries various lecture presentations that have been video-recorded from past events. The centre also holds copies of journals for the County Tipperary Historical Society, and a dedicated site at **www.tipperarylibraries. ie/ths/index.html** provides information on the contents for these from 1988 to 2010. The archive service for South Tipperary is located in

Clonmel, and its website at **www.southtipparchives.ie** provides basic details for its holdings.

An overview of Tipp's towns and villages can be found at **www.tipp.ie/townsandvillages.htm**. Tipperary Excel's website at **www.tfhr.org** has many useful boundary maps in its 'Advice' section, showing the various civil and ecclesiastic parishes, baronies, dioceses and more.

Connors Genealogy (**www.connorsgenealogy.com/tipp**) provides some interesting online transcriptions and documents, such as an alphabetical surname roster of emigrants, various townland maps, parish registers, and an index to those brought before the petty session court in Tipperary between 1851 and 1855. Griffith's Valuation (including original house books transcriptions), tithe records and some census records are also available. The Tipperary Irish genealogy project page at **www.igp-web.com/Tipperary** has an equally useful range of resources, including coroners' inquests from 1832 to 1877, some excellent cemetery pages (including Kilcommon's Quaker Cemetery), and trade directories from 1787, 1824, 1856 and 1889, as well as images from an undated Borough Guide to Clonmel. A list of Tipperary freeholders from 1776 is at **www.igp-web.com/Tipperary/freeholders/index.htm**.

Births from the year 1871 for Carrick-on-Suir can be found at **www.geocities.ws/irishancestralpages/cosbi1871.html**. For burial indexes in Ballinaclough, Barnane, Dovea (St Michael's), Drom (old and new cemeteries), Glenkeen, Ileigh, Inch, Kilfithmone, Kylanna, Loughmore, Powerstowns (now in County Waterford) and Templemore visit **http://members.webone.com.au/~sgrieves/cemetries__ireland.htm**.

Additional burials for Cahir, Clonmel and Cashel can also be found at **www.macatawa.org/~devries/Cemeteries.htm**.

As with Limerick, some War of Independence witness statements for Tipperary (sourced from the Bureau of Military History statements gathered in 1947) can be accessed via an interactive Google Map at **http://tinyurl.com/witnessstatements**. Brendan Hall's list of soldiers involved in the earlier 1856 mutiny of the North Tipperary Militia is available at **http://homepage.tinet.ie/~jbhall/index.html**. The Fame of Tipperary Group website at **http://homepage.tinet.ie/~tipperaryfame/** provides many essays on historical conflicts involving soldiers from Tipperary and beyond over the last 400 years.

A detailed list of Tipperary emigrants who sailed for New South Wales or Queensland between 1828 and 1866 is available at **http:// freepages.genealogy.rootsweb.ancestry.com/~maddenps/TIPPEM5.htm**.

Waterford

Waterford County Council's Library Service has a portal at **www.waterfordcountylibrary.ie** providing access to a library catalogue, and sections for 'Local Studies' and 'Family History'. Among the former you will find such gems as digitised editions of the *Dungarvan Leader* newspaper from 1918 to 1979 (browse only), aerial photographs of the county, a gazetteer database entitled 'Waterford Places' at **http://places. waterfordcountylibrary.ie** with translations of Irish/English place names, a townland index, various e-publications, and more. In the 'Family History' section you can gain access to databases on death registers from 1864 to 1901, graveyard inscriptions, Griffith's Valuation for the county, and various trade directories from 1824 to 1910.

The county archive service at **www.waterfordcoco.ie** also has a page with several downloadable guides for its holdings, and some great online exhibitions and projects, most notably the 'Lismore Estate Papers Emigration Record Database 1815–1905'. Waterford County Museum is equally on the ball at **www.waterfordcountymuseum.org**, with a list of mayors from 1377 to 1891 and a superb photographic database called Waterford County Image Archive, which is also accessible at **www.waterfordcountyimages.org**.

Waterford Historic Maps, courtesy of the council's library service.

Waterford City's archive service at **www.waterfordcity.ie/departments/ archives/news.htm** provides a broad overview of its collections, which include harbour board records, Quaker materials and maternity hospital records. A list of articles in the Waterford Archaeological and Historical Society can be found at **www.iol.ie/~mnoc/forHSoc.html**.

A 1912 *Parochial History of Waterford and Lismore during the 18th and 19th centuries* is online through the Internet Archive at **http://archive.org/ details/parochialhistory00nhar**. A much earlier work from 1824, *The History, Topography and Antiquities of the County and City of Waterford; with an Account of the Present State of the Peasantry of that part of the South of Ireland* is also available at **http://archive.org/details/historytopograph 00ryla**.

For a brief history of Dungarvan visit **www.dungarvan.com/ history.htm**, and for Lismore visit **www.discoverlismore.com**.

Chapter 7

CONNACHT

Also sometimes recorded as 'Connaught', the province of Connacht lies to the west of Ireland and contains the counties of Galway, Leitrim, Mayo, Roscommon and Sligo. It is Ireland's smallest province, with just over half a million residents today, with the largest settlement being the city of Galway. Despite its small size, many useful resources for the province are available online.

Galway

Some maps and tithe applotment records for Galway can be found at **www.connorsgenealogy.net/galway** along with a list of flax growers from 1796, some parish records for Loughrea Cathedral, Shanaglish parish and burials from Menlough Cemetery, and various extracts from Griffith's Valuation. A Little Bit of Ireland at **http://celticcousins.net/ireland/** also carries various parish records, will extracts, electoral lists, directories and more for the county, while the County Galway page on Genealogy Links has further offerings at **www.genealogylinks.net/uk/ireland/galway/index.html**.

Galway County Council Archives provides a very well described list of resources that it holds at **www.galway.ie/en/Services/Library/Archives**, covering everything from poor law union and council collections to various private papers held by the facility. Some of the downloadable guides are superb, for example those concerning Galway hospitals from 1802 to 1892, while the archive also has an online catalogue at **http://apps.galwaycoco.ie/adlib/Default.aspx**. The county's library service also has some useful offerings at **www.galwaylibrary.ie**, including the relevant 6-inch Ordnance Survey maps from 1842, a bilingual townland query system and an online catalogue.

Galway History (**www.galwayhistory.info**) has several essays, pictures and old movie clips concerning the county; there is also a Facebook page at **www.facebook.com/GalwayHistoryinfo**. For various old photos of Galway, postcards and even some old school magazines, visit **www.oldgalwaypics.co.uk**.

A Galway election list from 1727 is available at **www.celticcousins.net/ireland/galway1727.htm**.

Roots Ireland has a couple of Roman Catholic religious censuses for Kinarva in 1834 and for Spiddal in both 1884 and 1895. If your ancestors were from Lawrencetown then visit **www.lawrencetown.com** for some information on local families, the old school and more. A baptismal register for the Catholic parish of Woodford / Looscaune from 1865 to 1889 is freely available at **http://homepages.rootsweb.ancestry.com/~egan/baptismalrecords.htm**, along with a useful townland map and history for the area.

Finally, Connemara's Glengowla Silver and Lead site at **http://glengowla.goegi.com** recalls the history of the mine, which was abandoned in 1865, and includes a video tour of the facility.

Leitrim

The Leitrim–Roscommon Genealogy Website at **www.leitrim-roscommon.com** is a useful portal for various online collections for the county. The map page alone is well worth a visit at **www.leitrim-roscommon.com/LR_maps.html** for detailed parish and townland maps across the county. Connors Genealogy has a page at **www.connorsgenealogy.net/Leitrim** which includes various land records and useful English census records databases from 1851 to 1871, listing individuals who have given Leitrim as their place of birth.

The County Library's platform at **www.leitrimlibrary.ie** (also **www.leitrimcoco.ie/eng/Services_A-Z/Library**) has a searchable 'Local Studies' database carrying an index to all books, periodicals and files, as well as a newspaper database covering 1822 to 1905. An equally useful resource on the site is the 1830 list of townlands recorded by John O'Donovan for the Ordnance Survey, with both English and original Gaelic versions listed by civil parish.

Some headstone inscriptions from Dromahair, Glenade and Glencar can be found at **http://homepage.eircom.net/~kevm/index.htm**, with Church of Ireland cemetery inscriptions for Lurganboy and Manorhamilton available at **http://members.webone.com.au/~sgrieves/cemetries_ireland.htm#BARNANE**.

For a description of the state of Leitrim's agriculture in 1837 visit **www.libraryireland.com/topog/L/Leitrim-Agriculture.php**.

Mayo

Mayo County Library has a competent site at **www.mayolibrary.ie** filled with many resources including a clan map for the county, an exhibition guide on the region's Famine experience, a superb collection of online historic estate maps, and detailed guides to various Local Studies department holdings. An exploration of Mayo's history can be consulted at **www.mayohistory.com**, while a series of recorded podcast programmes on Mayo's Heritage, derived from tours of the county in 2007 and 2008, are at **www.podcasts.ie/weekly-shows/mayos-heritage**.

Parish records for Ballysakeery, Belmullet, Parke, Louisburgh, Bohola and Lacken, as well as various Mayo maps and land records, are online at **www.connorsgenealogy.net/Mayo**. The north-east of the county, particularly around Ballycastle, is covered by **www.goldenlangan.com**, and among several useful facilities there is an excellent graveyard list and locations page, with many headstones photographed.

Baptism indexes from Glenduff from 1872 to 1879 can be found at **http://archiver.rootsweb.ancestry.com/th/read/IRELAND/1997-11/08793 59579**, while transcriptions of burials at Killeen, Burrishoole, Kilmeena,

The history of the Marian shrine at Knock carries the witness statements of those who claimed to see the apparitions.

Aughavale, Murrisk, and Slievemore, with photos of headstones, are available at **www.bernieworld.net/cemeteries/The_Cemetery_Collection. htm**, along with a list of burial grounds located across Mayo. For Burrishoole you can also visit **http://reocities.com/Heartland/Park/ 7461/graves.html**, and several other cemeteries are found transcribed at a page entitled Irish Roots at **http://freepages.genealogy.rootsweb. ancestry.com/~deesegenes**, along with various lists drawn from civil registration records, parish registers and other useful resources.

A Little Bit of Ireland at **http://celticcousins.net/ireland/** has wills lists for Mayo, directory listings for Ballina and Killala, and some Church of Ireland parish material for Crossmolina from 1768 to 1803. Baptisms (1861–1880) and marriages (1835–1862) for Kiltimagh can be found at **www.rootsweb.ancestry.com/~fianna/transcript/index.html**.

Finally, the history of the Marian Shrine at Knock is explored at **www.knock-shrine.ie**, including a downloadable PDF file containing fifteen witness accounts of the apparitions of the Virgin Mary, and Saints Joseph and John, said to have appeared there in August 1879.

Roscommon

The Library section of Roscommon County Council's site at **www.roscommoncoco.ie** provides an overview of some of the Local Studies Centre's holdings in Roscommon, as well as an online catalogue for the library service's books.

The Leitrim–Roscommon Genealogy Website at **www.leitrim- roscommon.com** has various online collections for the county. A database of deaths from Roscommon Town Workhouse from the mid-1800s to the end of the century is available at **http://reocities.com/Heartland/ Pines/7030/page2.html**. At the time of writing, however, this only recorded surnames from A to D, with the link to subsequent pages seemingly broken or yet to be uploaded. Transcriptions of cemetery burials for Athleague Old Cemetery, St John's Lecarrow (New Cemetery) and Kilcommon Cemetery, Lecarrow, and other resources can be accessed at **www.roscommonhistory.ie/Genealogy/genealogyhome.htm**.

Several cemeteries have been transcribed for the Roscommon Irish Genealogy Projects website at **www.igp-web.com/roscommon**, and many photographs taken for the site's separate 'Headstones' category. The site is also useful for a list of landowners from the county in the 1870s, Royal Irish Constabulary officers from 1840 to 1853 and emigrant lists from Ballykilcline. The story of Ballykilcline, its evictions, emigration and more, is explored at **www.ballykilcline.com**.

The Arigna Mining Experience website at **www.arignamining experience.ie** has a detailed history section providing the background to the coal-mining operation near Carrick-on-Shannon which closed in 1990 after 400 years.

The Irish National Famine Museum at Strokestown Park has various resources online at **www.strokestownpark.ie/famine-museum/archive-papers**, including lists of meal distribution and emigrants from 1842 to 1848.

Various items of documentary ephemera as collected by Liam Byrne of South Roscommon can be viewed at **www.roscommonhistory.ie/Source.html**.

Sligo

Sligo County Libraries at **www.sligolibrary.ie/sligolibrarynew** has online catalogues to both its library and archive holdings, and many useful resources in its 'Local Studies' section, including some digitised online holdings within its 'General Guide to Collection' category. This includes an online mapping page for the 1837 6-inch first edition of the Ordnance Survey and the 1659 Downs Survey map of County Sligo, both of which are now represented on a platform known as 'Mapbrowser'. The navigation is a bit fiddly, so this can be directly accessed at **www.sligolibrary.ie/sligolibrarynew/LocalStudies/GeneralGuideto Collection/DigitalCollections/OnlineMapCollection**. It is fair to say that it is not particularly intuitive to use, but stick with it as the results are worth it – the 1659 parish maps in particular are beautiful. A page also celebrating the 400th anniversary of the creation of Sligo town's status as a borough in 2013 is also well worth a look at **www.sligolibrary.ie/sligolibrarynew/LocalStudies/Sligoe400/**.

Several published histories of Sligo town and county from the nineteenth century are freely available on the Internet Archive at **www.archive.org**, including works by Terence O'Rorke and W.G. Wood-Martin. A parish map for the county is online at **www.sligoroots.com/sources/county-sligo-parish-map**. Historic photographs from Sligo have also been placed online by Jim McSharry on a Picasa photo album at **http://tinyurl.com/jimmcsharrysligopics**.

The Sligo heritage project at **www.sligoheritage.com** has many fascinating articles on aspects of the county's history within its archive section, including essays on Constance Markievicz, the 1798 rebellion, the famine and more. K.P. Murray's Shamrock Cottage website at **http://homepage.eircom.net/~kevm/index.htm** details burials indexes for Ahamlish, Ballinakill and Sooey, Ballygawley, Banada Abbey, Calry, Carrigans, Curry, Drumcliffe, Keelogues, Kilmacowen, Killery, Lisadell, Rathcormack, Rosses Point, Scarden and Thurlestrane. Photographs can be requested of individual burial plots and stones. The site also carries information on Ships and Sailors of Sligo, including dates of wrecks.

Chapter 8

LEINSTER

Leinster is by far the most urbanised and populated province of Ireland, with the city of Dublin alone having over a million inhabitants. The province also contains the largest number of counties, namely Carlow, Dublin, Kildare, Kilkenny, Laois, Longford, Louth, Meath, Offaly, Westmeath, Wexford and Wicklow.

The following resources may further help with research in each county.

Carlow

The County Archives page of the Carlow Libraries website (**www.carlowlibraries.ie**) hosts details of several photographic collections as well as catalogues of small collections, the county's Grand Jury records and various family papers (e.g. the family papers of the Burtons of Burton Hall, 1570–1902). The Local History section provides details of holdings for maps, periodicals, newspapers and other genealogical resources, as well as several downloadable guides on how to commence your research and about the history of the county.

Susie Warren's County Carlow website at **http://home.people.net.au/~ousie/county_carlow_information.htm** dates back to 1999 and is packed with free to access transcribed datasets for the county. These range from 1659 census entries and trade directories, to memorial inscriptions and newspaper extracts. An absent voters list for Carlow, listing soldiers missing from the Register of Electors from 1920 to 1921, is available at **http://tinyurl.com/absentvoterscarlow**.

The Carlow County Museum site at **www.carlowcountymuseum.com** holds some interesting essays on topics such as archaeology, industry, sport and transport within the county, and on Carlow town itself. A list of Carlow- and Wexford-based Roman Catholic families preparing to emigrate in 1817 can be found at **www.theshipslist.com/ships/passengerlists/emigrants1818rc.shtml**.

A useful page on merchants of Tullow in 1824 is available at **www.rootsweb.ancestry.com/~irlcar2/tullow.htm**, which includes many shop postcards of the town from about 1910.

Dublin

Many of the national repositories for the Republic of Ireland, and indeed some for the whole of Ireland, are held in Dublin City, and as such have been described throughout the book, most notably the National Archives of Ireland and the National Library of Ireland on various pages. The National Museum of Ireland also provides details on its offerings at **www.museum.ie**, while the GAA Archive site at **www.crokepark.ie/gaa-museum/gaa-archive** describes its vast collections.

For the county of Dublin itself, the county council established in 1898 was replaced in 1993 by three new council authorities for Fingal, South Dublin and Dún Laoghaire-Rathdown. The records for the pre-1993 administration were handed over to Fingal County Council and maintained by its archive service, with funding for their preservation offered by the three replacements councils. On the county council site at **www.fingalcoco.ie** go through the 'Community and Recreation' tab to the 'Library' section, and then select 'Fingal Local Studies and Archive Service'. Once in, you will have two further options, to select 'Fingal Archives' or 'Fingal Local Studies'. The Archive section provides access to separate digitised collections, *Balbriggan Town Council Archived Minutes 1860–2010* (also accessible via **www.digisearch.ie/balbriggan/menu.asp**) and a *Fingal List Roll of Honour (WW1)*. The Local Studies page provides access to an oral history collection hosted on YouTube at **www.youtube.com/user/fingallocalstudies**, as well as a Postcard and Photograph Collection hosted on Flickr at **www.flickr.com/photos/fingallocalstudies**. As well as a catalogue, the Library's main area has an 'Online Database' page, which offers free access to the London-based *Times Digital Archive 1785–1985*.

Dún Laoghaire-Rathdown's county library site is at **www.dlrcoco.ie/library/index.html** and offers little more than a catalogue and Local History section, which includes a brief history of Dún Laoghaire. South Dublin County Libraries has a guide to its family history resources at **www.southdublinlibraries.ie/local-studies**, many historic photographs at **http://source.southdublinlibraries.ie** and some excellent historic maps at **http://gis.sdublincoco.ie/historical_mapping/** – these go as far back as 1760, with the site also including aerial photography from 2009. The council also provides access to these maps via a great site entitled 'Our

Villages' at **www.southdublinhistory.ie**, which also includes a detailed overview and history for the main settlements in the south of Dublin.

The Dublin City Public Libraries and Archives platform at **www.dublincity.ie/recreationandculture/libraries/pages/DublinCityLibrary.aspx** is packed with goodies, from a library catalogue and blog to a section entitled 'Heritage and History'. The home page for the latter category offers interesting resources such as image collections and even a diary of Dublin-based weather from 1714 to 1716. On the left of the page are various sub-categories, such as the 'Dublin and Irish Collections', 'Dublin City Archives' and 'Family History'. The archive site has a series of collections concerning the history of the city from the twelfth century to those for specific subjects, such as the Irish Theatre Archive, the Royal Dublin Fusiliers Archive, the Dublin City Archaeological Archive and Dublin City Sports Archive, each of which has an adequate description. The 'Family History' section contains details of the facility's many holdings.

The library page also links to the excellent Dublin Heritage project (**www.dublinheritage.ie**), which contains free to access electoral lists for the city from 1939 to 1940, a directory of Dublin graveyards, and a database of the Ancient Freemen of Dublin. Additional resources include

The Dublin Heritage website.

'Historic Postcards', 'Historical Maps' and a 'Dublin Diary' of events from the city's past. A list of family and local history societies is available at **www.dublinheritage.ie/associations/index.htm,** which is well worth exploring – the Finglas Historical Society, for example, has brilliant 'History' and 'Photographs' sections, while the Mount Merrion Historical Society site leads you to the Mount Merrion 300 site at **www.mountmerrion300.ie**, commemorating 300 years of the area in Dún Laoghaire-Rathdown County.

Trish Loughman's Dublin 1850 site at **www.dublin1850.com** is another heroic contribution to the history of the county and city, with lists of former Dublin Lord Mayors, trade directory entries, photos and more. A transcript of St Mary's Roman Catholic Cemetery inscriptions in Howth is available at **http://freepages.genealogy.rootsweb.ancestry.com/~chrisu/howth/howthcem.htm**.

Kildare

Kildare County Council Library's Kildare Collections and Research Services page (**www.kildare.ie/Library/KildareCollectionsandResearchServices/**) offers an overview to both its Genealogy and County Archive services. The 'Services' and 'Resources' tab provides various guides and free databases for research, such as one listing freeholders and leaseholders from 1835 to 1839. You will also find a detailed account of the Great War in Kildare, coverage of the All Ireland Football Championship from across 1928, and much more. The library service's County Kildare Online Electronic History Journal at **www.kildare.ie/library/ehistory** is essentially a blog that hosts various additional transcribed resources, articles and links to useful sites. The *Kildare Observer* newspaper from 1880 to 1935 is hosted on the pay-per-view Irish Newspaper Archives site, but thanks to the county council can also in fact be accessed for free via **http://tinyurl.com/9f678ny**.

A project from Kildare Community Network on the commemorations of the 1798 rebellion in both 1898 and 1948 can be accessed at **www.kildare.ie/employment/fas/cytpprofiles/leader/1798/1798.htm**, while a list of First World War casualties from Kildare is available at **www.esatclear.ie/~curragh/casualty.htm**.

Kilkenny

Kilkenny County Council's Library Service page (**www.kilkennycoco.ie**) provides access to a site for its Local Studies collections. There is a downloadable leaflet entitled *Local Studies and Genealogical Resources*, and guides to many of its local holdings in its archives, on microfilm and in print, with several examples. Two trade directories are also available for download, both from 1884: the *Kilkenny City and County Guide and Directory* and *The Illustrated Guide City and County of Kilkenny* (located in the 'Historic Publications' page).

If you are interested in how to survey field names for a particular parish, the Townlands site at **www.townlands.net** provides a free guide on how this was accomplished in the civil parish of Rathcoole.

An interesting thesis by T.G. Fewer, entitled *Women and personal possessions: 17th-century testamentary evidence from counties Waterford and Kilkenny, Ireland* can be read at **www.assemblage.group. shef.ac.uk/3/3fewer.htm**.

Various transcribed resources for the county can be accessed at **www.connorsgenealogy.com/Kilkenny**, including Roman Catholic parish baptisms (1812–1870) and marriages (1834–1867) for Castlecomer, as well as for Conahy (1833–1873), and a list of property lost by Castlecomer residents during the 1798 rebellion. For the history of coal mining in Castlecomer visit **www.sip.ie/sip019B/index1.htm**.

Finally, Kilkenny Archaeological Society's website at **http://kilkenny archaeologicalsociety.ie** contains a list of all articles to have been published in its journal, the *Old Kilkenny Review*.

Laois (Queen's County)

Laois County Council's Local research portal at **www.laois.ie/ LeisureandCulture/Libraries/LocalResearch** provides links to four sections: 'Laois Archives', 'Local History Online', 'Local Studies' and 'Genealogy', though all are extremely basic at the time of writing.

Irish Midlands Ancestry (**www.irishmidlandsancestry.com**) includes many parish histories from the county, biographies on various famous folk, maps and old photos. Of particular interest is the 'A–Z of Laois', which essentially reproduces Samuel Lewis's Topographical Dictionary of the county from 1837. Several database resources for Laois can be found at **www.connorsgenealogy.com/Leix**, including various parish registers and land records. A considerably more detailed site for the south-east of the county is the Brennan Family History project at **http://freepages.family.rootsweb.ancestry.com/~mjbrennan/index.htm**. It includes a Laois Surname Registry listing the research interest of many in the county. Freeholders from Laois from 1758 to 1775 are listed online at **www.igp-web.com/laois/freeholders.htm**.

The Donaghmore Famine Workhouse Museum website at **www. donaghmoremuseum.com** provides a case study on one of the inmates there in 1859–1860, as well as old photos and the story of the Donaghmore Co-operative Movement established in 1889.

A great place to browse for images and old documents on Portlaoise can be found at **www.portlaoisepictures.com/index.html**.

Longford

Longford County Library's site (**www.longfordlibrary.ie**) has very brief listings of holdings on its 'Local Studies', 'Genealogy' and 'Irish Studies' pages, but the 'Archives' section provides more detailed information on its local authority archives and private papers collections. The site also catalogues many of its estate maps and townland maps. Another useful asset on the site is the place names section, which lists various parishes, baronies and townlands. At the time of writing, it also offered a search facility for the dataset, but this was found to not be working, so place descriptions could be browsed only.

The Heritage section of the website has many useful guides on churchyards and field monuments which may also be of interest, including *The Care and Conservation of Graveyards*, and *Guidelines for the Care and Conservation of Historic Graveyards*, both containing much good advice, particularly if you wish to survey a burial ground in your area.

The Internet Archive hosts a copy of *History of the County of Longford* by James P. Farrell at **http://archive.org/details/cu31924028071029**, first published in 1891.

Louth

The website for the county archive for Louth (**www.louthcoco.ie/ en/Services/Archives**) has some wonderfully detailed pages on its collections. Not only does the site provide some much-needed context to the records, it even tells you how to look for them in its online catalogue, in one of the most user-friendly archive sites online. In addition there is a handy 'Document of the Month' feature, and a section allowing users to download publications and research guides on topics such as house history, crew lists and passenger lists. The catalogue (directly accessible at **http://193.178.1.203/adlib**) maintains this friendliness, allowing users to retrieve previous searches via a 'Search History' function, and to download search results in Microsoft Word format. There is also a great genealogy section, which offers considerably more than just the basics of family history.

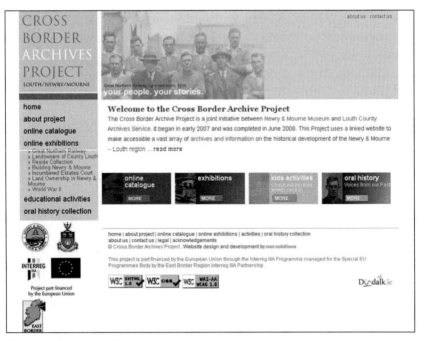

The Cross Border Archive Project.

The Cross Border Archives Project at **www.louthnewryarchives.ie** (see p. 117) contains information on landowners of Louth from 1854, including an interactive map identifying the locations of holdings, and the Encumbered Estates Court proceedings in the county. The site also holds recordings made for the Louth Oral History Project, and provides access to Louth County Archives online catalogue.

Brendan Hall's *County Louth Genealogical Resources* site at **www.jbhall.freeservers.com/index.html** has an extraordinary collection of transcribed resources, including militia lists, directories, voter lists, petitions and statistical surveys of parishes, and some fascinating essays on localised incidents such as the 1816 Murders at Wildgoose Lodge.

For all things Battle of the Boyne visit **www.battleoftheboyne.ie**, where the 'Battle and Beyond' section provides an interesting oversight of various subjects concerning the Williamite campaign in 1690. The Drogheda Museum at Millmount, an old Martello Tower, has a website at **www.millmount.net** with some basic online guides to subjects such as the Post Office in Drogheda. At the time of writing the site had an irritating problem whereby several menu features from the drop-down menu were covered by photographs lower down the page, rendering them inaccessible – but the site's search function brings up such pages on archaeology, geology, the history of the Post Office and Drogheda's rowing club.

The parish of Faughart is well catered for by its historical society at **www.faughart.com**, with the site offering details of graveyard burials at Ballmascanlon, Bridge-a-Crin, Castletown, Faughart, Kane, Kilcurry and Urney. Lists of freeholders from 1822 and 1824/5 can be found at **www.rootsweb.ancestry.com/~fianna/transcript/index.html**, alongside a list of Dundalk householders from 1837, Tullyallen New Church subscribers, and tenants of Lord Roden from 1837.

Meath

The Meath County Council Library Service site, found within the council's Community pages at **www.meath.ie**, has very basic 'Genealogy' and 'Local Studies' sections, providing little more than an overview of material held at the Library Headquarters in Navan.

A list of Roman Catholic parishes in Meath is available on the Fianna page at **www.rootsweb.ancestry.com/~fianna/county/meath/mearc.html**, with a page of some published resources, such as monumental inscriptions and trade directories, at **www.rootsweb.ancestry.com/~fianna/county/meath/mea-1.html**. The County Meath Ireland Genealogy project at **www.rootsweb.ancestry.com/~irlmea** includes emigration lists, people from Meath in the 1870 and 1880 US censuses, and in the 1901 English census. A small number of parish and cemetery records are also listed, as well as a census of Meath drawn up under the authority of Bishop Thomas Lewis O' Beirne in 1802, transcribed and arranged by parish at **http://tinyurl.com/Meath1802**.

For Ashbourne and south-eastern Meath, visit **www.angelfire. com/ak2/ashbourne**. This hosts general information on researching family history in the county, but also some useful resources such as a list of children who studied at Ashbourne National School between 1870 and 1906.

Offaly (King's County)

The Local Studies and Archive Service section of Offaly County Council's website at **www.offaly.ie** provides nothing more than a very basic overview to its services and holdings, though it does give a good list of newspapers and their coverage available at the library's headquarters in Tullymore.

Irish Midlands Ancestry (**www.irishmidlandsancestry.com**) has a section of its site devoted to the county, including a gazetteer, maps of the county from 1837 and 1881, a community history, a guide to some of its more famous sons and daughters and a list (unsourced) of some inhabitants from the nineteenth century.

Offaly Historical and Archaeological Society (**www.offalyhistory.com**) has a couple of newspaper articles from 2011 describing Moneygall in 1800, and on Board of Works supervisor John Keegan's diary of South Offaly during the Famine.

The history of some of Offaly's towns is described at **http://ireland. iol.ie/~offaly/tull.htm**.

Westmeath

Westmeath County Council is online at **www.westmeath.coco.ie**. Its Library Service has a few items of interest, including a section entitled 'Westmeath in the Past', which offers several downloadable history guides on subjects such as the county's inland waterways, the railways, the Westmeath Hunt and Belvedere House. The service's Local Studies is packed with detailed listings of the library's genealogical resources, newspaper holdings, folklore collections and even a page detailing the connections between Westmeath and Argentina.

Various indexes to parish records and Griffith's Valuation for Ballynacargy can be found on a South African-based site at **www.ancestorfind.net/index-11.html**. Some headstone records from Killafree at Castlepollard can be found at **http://interment.net/data/ ireland/westmeath/killafree/killafree.htm**. A site for Athlone's story, including a useful reading list and essays on several topics, can be found at **www.athlone.ie/History**.

James Woods' Annals of Westmeath, published in 1907, can be found on the Internet Archive at **http://archive.org/details/annalsofwestmeat 00wooduoft**. James Murphy's 1913 work *Convict No. 25; or, the Clearances of Westmeath: a story of the Whitefeet*, is also available on the site at **http://archive.org/details/convictno25orcle00murprich**.

Wexford

The Library pages of Wexford County Archive's site at **www.wexford.ie** include a library catalogue and a series of oral history podcasts, with anecdotes from 130 interviewees from 2008 onwards. You can search by name or by an area of interest, choosing from Enniscorthy, Gorey, New

Ross or Wexford. The site also provides detailed descriptions of its holdings in its 'Local Studies' area, though no online databases or collections.

The County Archive section of the website is similarly presented, with many detailed guides to the holdings available at the facility in Ardcavan. This does present some digitised and transcribed material online, however, in the form of estate papers for Lord Templemore's estate of Dunbrody Park, Arthurstown. These are mainly maps of the estate, though also some listings of tenants.

For histories of both Wexford county and the city visit **www.rootsweb.ancestry.com/~irlwex2/history.html**. A list of Irish emigrants from the county to New York from 1846 to 1851 can be located at **www.rootsweb.ancestry.com/~irlwex2/wexford_immigrants.html**. The Ships List also provides a list of Carlow and Wexford families preparing to emigrate in 1817 at **www.theshipslist.com/ships/ passengerlists/emigrants1818rc.shtml**.

An account of Wexford's part in the 1798 United Irishmen rebellion can be found on the Internet Archive at **http://archive.org/details/ warinwexfordacco00whee**, through a book published in 1910 entitled *The War in Wexford: an Account of the Rebellion in the South of Ireland in 1798.*

Wicklow

Wicklow County Council's Archive service has its own dedicated webpage at **www.wicklow.ie/archives,** though the site offers very little other than a brief description of some of its collections, as well as links to neighbouring archive services in adjacent counties. The county's family history centre site at **www.wicklow.ie/familyhistorycentre** is similarly sparse with its online offerings.

A database for those who swore an oath to the United Irishmen in the county from 1797 to 1804 is available at **http://members.pcug.org.au/ ~ppmay/wicklow.htm**. A Rebel Hand is a fascinating website at **http://rebelhand.weebly.com** which recalls the story of Nicholas Delaney, who was sentenced to death for his participation in the 1798 Rebellion, but whose sentence was commuted to transportation to New South Wales. For the history of Wicklow Gaol visit **www.wicklows historicgaol.com/history.htm**.

Chapter 9

THE IRISH DIASPORA

When pursuing Irish ancestral research it helps to discover what happened to members of the family who might have emigrated, for where gaps in the Irish records might appear, those in an adopted homeland may well compensate. It can also be a source of great pride to discover the achievements of cousins in new lands facing different challenges to your own branch of the family – and to perhaps discover that while an accent or nationality may change over time, the blood certainly does not.

The connections with Britain have been well documented in this book, but the Moving Here website from the UK National Archives also has a category on Irish migration at **http://movinghere.org.uk/galleries/ histories/irish/irish.htm**.

Emigration

The Irish diaspora is huge and to this day maintains a strong connection to its ancestral homeland. The Documenting Ireland: Parliament, People and Migration (DIPPAM) project at **www.dippam.ac.uk** is a joint venture between Queen's University Belfast, the University of Ulster, the Centre for Migration Studies, and Libraries Northern Ireland. It provides a fascinating range of resources on emigration (primarily to North America) from the eighteenth to the twentieth century, including an 'Irish Emigration Database' with diaries, journals, folklore and newspaper extracts, and the 'Voices of Migration and Return' oral history project, with many audio recordings and transcripts of those who travelled. The Centre for Migration Studies based in Omagh has a comprehensive links page at **www.qub.ac.uk/cms/admin/links.htm** for additional resources, with some of its Irish Emigration Database records also available on the pay-per-view Roots Ireland site. The Irish Diaspora website (**www. irishdiaspora.net**) is another academic project from the University of

Leeds, with many diverse essays and links on various aspects to do with the study of the Irish abroad.

For passenger lists the FindmyPast UK website offers a useful starting point with its 'Passenger Lists Leaving UK 1890–1960' collection, sourced from the National Archives' Board of Trade records at Kew. This offers records for all those who sailed from British and Irish ports between 1890 and 1921, and British ports only from 1922 to 1960. The site also carries a separate 'Register of Passport Applications' from 1851 to 1856, 1858 to 1862 and 1874 to 1903. Note that travellers from the United Kingdom did not have to hold a passport until 1914, so these were granted upon request.

Not every passenger who sailed abroad remained, while some who did settle overseas made return trips – for these you can find a parallel set of records from 1890 to 1960 on Ancestry, via its 'UK Incoming Passenger Lists, 1878–1960' collection. Ancestry also hosts a great many additional resources for emigration, including immigration records, naturalisation papers, vital records and subsequent censuses for various countries, particularly the United States, Canada and Australia. FindmyPast Ireland also has the extremely useful 'Transatlantic Migration from North America to Britain & Ireland 1858–1870' database – a detailed background to the politics behind this collection is available at **http://tinyurl.com/transatlanticreturns**. The same database is offered at Irish Origins.

Further passenger lists for North America, Australia and New Zealand can be accessed via **www.germanroots.com/onlinelists.html** and at **www.theshipslist.com**. Additional lists from Ulster can also be found at **www.ulsterancestry.com/ua-free-pages.php**.

United States

Ellis Island in New York maintained an immigration centre from 1892 to 1954, with the first immigrant to pass through its doors being Cork-born lass Annie Moore. To search those who arrived from Ireland, visit **www.ellisisland.org**. An alternative way to search this database is to go through the JewishGen portal at **www.jewishgen.org/databases/EIDB**. For earlier arrivals to New York (between 1820 and 1892) you can try the centre's predecessor facility at Castle Garden, with a database at **www.castlegarden.org**.

For the Famine period, the US National Archives has two useful collections, the 'Famine Irish Passenger Record Data File 1846–51 (FIPAS)' and the 'List of Ships that Arrived at the Port of New York 1846–51', both of which can be consulted at **http://aad.archives.gov/aad/series-**

The former immigration centre at Ellis Island.

description.jsp?s=639&cat=all&bc=sl. An additional resource for the US Irish diaspora is the Irish Abroad website's 'Roots' page at **www.irish abroad.com/Irish-Roots**.

A general gateway site for United States resources is the US GenWeb site at **www.rootsweb.ancestry.com/usgenweb**. The Library of Congress Online Catalog at **http://catalog.loc.gov** can help to source many American publications, photos and media of interest, while the National Archives (**www.archives.gov**) has a great quantity of guides and resources on its site for genealogical research. For a list of state archives, visit **www.archives.gov/research/alic/reference/state-archives.html**, and a guide to state historical societies is found at **www.stenseth.org/us/statehs.html**.

The Irish Ancestral Research Association (TIARA) in Massachusetts may also be of help at **http://tiara.ie**. This hosts an online surname database for its members' interests, as well as providing inscriptions from several cemeteries in the state listing an Irish birthplace, and resources on the Massachusetts Catholic Order of Foresters.

Canada

Those who sailed to Canada faced additional hardships apart from the long journey by sea. At Grosse Île over 100,000 Irish migrants arrived in

1847 and endured a major outbreak of typhus, with well over 5,000 buried at the quarantine station. The story of the tragedy is at **www.pc.gc.ca/eng/lhn-nhs/qc/grosseile/natcul/natcul1/b.aspx**, and a memorial database can be found at **www.pc.gc.ca/eng/lhn-nhs/qc/grosseile/natcul/natcul4.aspx**.

Many other Canadian passenger lists and immigration resources can be found at the Library and Archives Canada site at **www.collectionscanada.gc.ca**, as well as a database of 'Home Children' who arrived in the country between 1869 and 1930. These were predominantly orphaned children sent by the British Government from the UK to new homes across its empire, though in some cases parents and children were misled as to the fate of the other prior to their separation. The database includes hundreds sent from poor law unions and charitable institutions in Ireland. A further resource for Canadian-destined Home Children is located at **http://freepages.genealogy. rootsweb.ancestry.com/~britishhomechildren**. The Child Migrants Trust (**www.childmigrantstrust.com**) helps many who were transported overseas in more recent times to re-establish contact with family members, including many from Northern Ireland.

Australia

The National Archives of Australia (**www.naa.gov.au**) offers a comprehensive online guide for tracing immigrants to its shores through its 'Family History' section, accessible from the home page. The country's National Library site (**www.nla.gov.au**) hosts a detailed guide also for all Australian state libraries and archives, as well as vital records access, cemeteries databases, convicts databases and more – access this through the 'Quicklinks' section at the bottom of the home page. The library's impressive Trove facility (**http://trove.nla.gov.au**) is also well worth searching, particularly for its millions of digitised images from newspapers across the continent. The Australian Dictionary of National Biography can be consulted at **http://adbonline.anu.edu.au**.

For convicts who were sent to Australia, the National Archives of Ireland has an 'Ireland–Australia Transportation database' featuring almost 39,000 Irish people at **www.nationalarchives.ie/research/ archives-held-in-the-national-archives/introduction/**, while Down County Museum's website (**www.downcountymuseum.com**) hosts two convicts databases of prisoners from the county who were transported to Australia.

Patricia Downes' Australian Pioneers site at **http://members.pcug. org.au/~pdownes** carries a list of Irish convicts sent to New South Wales from 1788 to 1849, and the State Library of Queensland's Convicts Transportation Registers database is available at **www.slq.qld.gov.au/info/fh/convicts/about**. FindmyPast UK has a 'Convict Arrivals in New South Wales 1788–1842' database, and The Genealogist also has several convicts-based resources including the names of Irish prisoners.

A blog for publishing company Irish Wattle may also be of interest at **http://irishwattle.blogspot.co.uk**.

New Zealand

The New Zealand Society of Genealogists' platform at **www.genealogy.org.nz** contains a 'Shipping Database' from 1840 to 1975 and a 'First Families Index' which can help you to pursue the earliest migrants to the country. Pearl's Pad (**http://pearlspad.net.nz**) equally has many historical resources for tracing migration, and PapersPast (**http://paperspast.natlib.govt.nz/cgi-bin/paperspast**) freely offers 2 million digitised newspaper pages from 1839 to 1945.

The New Zealand Government has a Births, Deaths and Marriages Online site at **www.bdmonline.dia.govt.nz** which provides indexes for historical vital events, namely births prior to a hundred years ago, marriages prior to eighty years ago and deaths prior to fifty years ago (or at least for those with a date of birth at least eighty years ago). Archives New Zealand has a catalogue on its site at **www.archway.archives.govt.nz** and includes access to details of New Zealand Defence Force records, some of which are digitised. The New Zealand History Online site at **www.nzhistory.net.nz** includes a war memorials register with some 450 sites listed. The Dictionary of New Zealand Biography has some 3,000 biographical entries at **www.dnzb.govt.nz**.

South America

An often forgotten part of Ireland's diaspora is that which settled in South America, but over 40,000 Irish people migrated there in the nineteenth century. Half moved on again to the US, Australia and elsewhere, but some 20,000 remained in Uruguay, Paraguay and Argentina, with their descendants today estimated to be around half a million strong. Among those to make their mark was the founder of the Argentinian Navy, William Brown, a Mayo man born in Foxford in 1777. The Society for Irish Latin American Studies has an excellent Dictionary of Latin American Biography at **www.irlandeses.org/bios1.htm** to help tell their story. Other resources on the site include passenger lists and detailed essays on the settlers' stories.

A late nineteenth-century postcard from Mary Gorman of Three Bridges, Kilkenny, and family.

Europe

The Irish in Europe (**http://irishineurope.ie/vre**) is a project hosted by the National University of Ireland at Maynooth, in County Kildare. The site contains four biographical databases of folk who worked in Europe, including 16,000 soldiers who served in the French army in the eighteenth century, a Spanish military database with 15,000 names, a University of Louvain database with 1,200 students from Ireland who studied there in the sixteenth to eighteenth centuries, and a similar database of 1,500 names for those who studied at the Universities of Paris and Toulouse.

Datasets coming soon include Irish naval personnel in French and Spanish service in the early modern period, Irish officers in the French Service in the eighteenth century, Irish law students at the Inns of Court in London during the seventeenth century, Irish medical students at the University of Rheims in the eighteenth century, and the Irish in Paris hospitals in the seventeenth and eighteenth centuries.

Ireland Reaching Out

And finally, do have a look at the Ireland Reaching Out project at **www.irelandxo.com**. It was initially established in Galway as a project to try to trace the diaspora, rather than have the diaspora try to trace folk in Ireland, but the concept is now spreading across the country. The site offers many resources including a forum to post interests and the chance to keep up-to-date with developments for your area of interest, as well as the annual Week of Welcomes. There is also a Facebook page at **www.facebook.com/IrelandXO**.

FURTHER READING

BARDON, Jonathan (1992) *A History of Ulster*. Belfast, Blackstaff Press

BLATCHFORD, R. and E. (2011, 2012) *The Irish Family and Local History Handbook (Vols 1 & 2)*. Robert Blatchford Publishing Ltd

CONNOLLY, S.J. (2011) *The Oxford Companion to Irish History*. Oxford, Oxford University Press

FOWLER, Simon (2006) *Tracing Your Army Ancestors*. Barnsley, Pen & Sword Books Ltd

FOX-DAVIES, Arthur (1978) *A Complete Guide to Heraldry*. New York, Bonanza Books

GRENHAM, John (2006) *Tracing Your Irish Ancestors*. Dublin, Gill & MacMillan Ltd

HERBER, Mark (2005) *Ancestral Trails*. Sparkford, Sutton Publishing Ltd

MAXWELL, Ian (2009) *How to Trace Your Irish Ancestors*. Barnsley, Pen & Sword Books Ltd

MAXWELL, Ian (2010) *Tracing Your Northern Irish Ancestors*. Barnsley, Pen & Sword Books Ltd

O'NEILL, Robert K. (2007) *Irish Libraries, Archives, Museums and Genealogical Centres*. Belfast, Ulster Historical Foundation

PATON, Chris (2011) *Tracing Your Family History on the Internet*. Barnsley, Family History Partnership

POMEROY, Chris (2007) *Family History in the Genes*. London, The National Archives

INDEX

Tracing Your Family History?

Read Your Family HISTORY

ESSENTIAL ADVICE FROM THE EXPERTS

FREE COPY!

Your Family History is the only magazine that is put together by expert genealogists. Our editorial team, led by Dr Nick Barratt, is passionate about family history, and our networks of specialists are here to give essential advice, helping readers to find their ancestors and solve those difficult questions.

In each issue we feature a **Beginner's Guide** covering the basics for those just getting started, a **How To** … section to help you to dig deeper into your family tree and the opportunity to **Ask The Experts** about your tricky research problems. We also include a **Spotlight** on a different county each month and a **What's On** guide to the best family history courses and events, plus much more.

Receive a free copy of *Your Family History* magazine and gain essential advice and all the latest news. To request a free copy of a recent back issue, simply e-mail your name and address to marketing@your-familyhistory.com or call 01226 734302*.

Your Family History is in all good newsagents and also available on subscription for six or twelve issues. For more details on how to take out a subscription, call 01778 392013 or visit **www.your-familyhistory.co.uk**.

Alternatively read issue 31 online completely free using this QR code

*Free copy is restricted to one per household and available while stocks last.